YOU GIVE ME NEW LIFE

Rekindling the Inner Fire Devotional Series

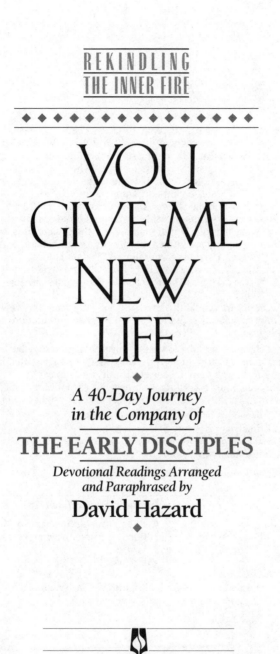

REKINDLING
THE INNER FIRE

* * * * * * * * * * * *

YOU GIVE ME NEW LIFE

*A 40-Day Journey
in the Company of*

THE EARLY DISCIPLES

*Devotional Readings Arranged
and Paraphrased by*

David Hazard

♦

BETHANY HOUSE PUBLISHERS
MINNEAPOLIS, MINNESOTA 55438
A Division of Bethany Fellowship, Inc.

Published by Bethany House Publishers
A Ministry of Bethany Fellowship, Inc.
11300 Hampshire Avenue South
Minneapolis, Minnesota 55438

Printed in the United States of America.

Library of Congress Cataloging-in-Publication Data

You give me new life : a 40-day journey in the company of
   the early disciples: devotional readings / arranged and
   paraphrased by David Hazard.
     p.   cm. — (Rekindling the inner fire.)

   1. Spiritual life—Catholic Church—Early works to
1800.   2. Meditations—Early works to 1800.
I. Hazard, David.   II. Series.
BX2178.Y68   1995
242—dc20   95–42404
ISBN 1–55661–677–5   CIP

To all the fine shepherds
of God's flock
who want to be found faithful
to the life-giving message
of Jesus Christ:

Be strong,
because we need you;
but rest in God,
because you need Him.

Contents

Foreword

*. . . our Savior . . . has destroyed death and has
brought our life and immortality to light. . . .*

---

2 Timothy 1:9–10

*T*heir names are strange to us: Athenagoras,
Ignatius, Polycarp. . . . Unfortunate, because these
men of the first and second centuries have been the
ones that I, a man of the twentieth century, turn to
when facing my greatest needs. Like the deathly
emptiness I felt some dozen years after I'd become
a Christian.

Inwardly, I was dry—as in *dying-of-thirst* dry.
Even my prayers were coming out parched: *Jesus,
you said if I believed in you, a river of living water would
flow within me. I do trust in you. But I'm so dead inside.*
Spiritually, I was mud and rocks in there. Not even
a trickle. . . .

I thought the problem was with God. With
Christianity. If we listened to our own prayers more
often—especially the bones we pick with God—

we'd find them far more descriptive of *us* than of Him. As Hannah Whitall Smith said, "God is not lost. We are."

So there I was: A Christian who looked spiritually well from the outside—in terms of church, service, Bible knowledge—but was inwardly more lost than found. I began to wonder, *What did Christians of the past know about a deeper relationship that I've missed?* Why would these people have given their lives for the Faith?—unless they'd found the promised *new life from above*, and it was so satisfying that nothing in this life could make them give up what they'd discovered.

I tell this personal story, only because you can mistake a love for the classic writings of the early Christians as a purely intellectual exercise. But there's no way you can read the works of these men—men who were led into Christ by Paul, John, and the other apostles—and not be captured by their passion for Christ, their sense of awe at His real, constant presence with them, and also their fierce pastoral care of the new Church.

So in this, the ninth REKINDLING THE INNER FIRE devotional, I feel privileged to bring you the faith, zeal, plain common sense, and spiritual wisdom of the men who took the Church from the hands of the apostles, shepherding it through a dark and dangerous world. These men, known as the *Apostolic Fathers* could not turn from Christ even in the face of persecution and torture—because they'd tasted the *Life*. And by comparison this world became pulp.

Let me introduce you to the men who will help you find your way deeper into that river of new life that comes to us from above. Beginning with Paul's companion, and his work. . . .

Barnabas. The *Letter of Barnabas* was among the sacred Scriptures read throughout the early Church, and it dates from late in the first century. No one then doubted it was penned by Paul's famous traveling companion, but the author never signed his name to the document. And so by the fourth century, when it was necessary to protect the Church from heretical forgeries, Athanasius, Jerome, and others made the hard decision to drop the *Letter* from the canon.

The writer, however, stands dead-center in the stream of Jesus' and the apostles' teaching: Life in the Spirit is not a matter of outward duties and ritual, as if we're still "buying" God's approval—instead the true believer's actions flow out from change in the inner man. God looks on the heart.

Ignatius of Antioch. In A.D. 69, he succeeded Barnabas as second overseer of one of the most important centers of early Christianity. His passion for Christ is as fiery as his name suggests. Undoubtedly, he absorbed a certain inner fire by sitting under the teachings of Paul, who had recently been martyred.

When he wrote the letters we have from him, his arms were weighted with chains. Between A.D. 98 and 117, the Emperor Trajan decided this gentle old man was dangerous and had him arrested. The crowds in Rome's colosseum saw him torn apart by wild beasts for their afternoon's pleasure. Men from various churches had been sent to accompany Ignatius—our great fortune—and they brought letters from his hand to five congregations. Also one to his young friend, the bishop Polycarp.

He loved Christ so much and longed to be with Him: Listen to him plead with the churches, begging them not to do anything to prevent his death—"Let me be ground like wheat by the wild beasts!" He wanted only to follow Jesus through the door of martyrdom into life eternal. His boldness tells us we are the losers, we who cling to our worldly possessions and comforts.

Polycarp of Smyrna. The intensely devoted pupil of the Apostle John, Polycarp (ca. A.D. 69–155) knew many who had seen Jesus in the flesh. So holy was his life that those he served as bishop in Smyrna actually vied to wait on him— claiming that sometimes when they touched him, healing virtue came from God and took away their sicknesses.

"Play the man, Polycarp!" rang a voice from heaven, as he was led into the colosseum to be burned alive. But this wasn't the only miracle that occurred during this eighty-six-year-old martyr's death, as you'll read.

Justin Martyr. The son of Roman colonists in Samaria, Justin (ca. A.D. 100–165) prepared for a career in philosophy—big business in those days. When he was about thirty, he met an old man while walking along a seashore. "Ask God to open the gates of spiritual light for you," the man told Justin, "for you can never perceive God, or know His truths, unless the Spirit of God enlightens you."

"When he walked away," Justin wrote later, "my spirit was set on fire. . . . His was the only useful philosophy I had ever found." He was converted almost on the spot.

The Romans and Greeks were dismissing this "new religion" of the Christians: In their attacks, Justin found his sacred calling. He opened a philosophical school in Rome, debating angry pagans who wanted the Christians rooted out. In his "apologies"—the first written defenses of the Faith—he showed how the *Logos* in fact planted the light of reason in all men everywhere, so that we would recognize Him when He walked among us, incarnate: So the pagan myths, and stories of the zodiac, gave "shadows" of the truth—by which the pagans were to recognize Truth when He came. We find his thought-currents streaming through the later works of Athenagoras, Irenaeus, and Tatian.

Praised for his holy, heroic life, Justin inflamed the pagans with his appeals to abandon their outmoded and decaying religion, and for that he was beheaded about A.D. 165.

The Didache. This early teaching tract was an attempt, it seems, to condense the teaching of Jesus and the apostles into short-form. Probably, it originated in a Christian community in Egypt or Syria, and it was in wide circulation by about A.D. 120. Athanasius would highly recommend it as a good tonic for all new converts. Also known as "The Two Roads," the *Didache* warns us to choose the Way of Life in Christ over the pathway of death, in very practical terms. The entry used here warns Christians in "the last days" to keep the inner fire of faith burning as we await Christ's return.

By now, all the apostles were gone. For men like Ignatius, Polycarp, and Justin Martyr, every living moment was borrowed time. Who would lead the Church when the Roman guard dragged *them* away? It couldn't be left to doctrinaire Christians only—leadership had to come from those who had been filled with the "new life from above."

So those who were discipled at the feet of the apostles took Paul's admonition to heart, pouring their lives into a new rank of godly young men. Enter a new generation. . . .

Tatian the Assyrian (ca. A.D. 110–172) was a prized student of Justin Martyr—and a man whose zeal went too far. A good warning for us, because even the most well-meaning Christians can go out of balance by focusing on just one aspect of the spiritual life. Tatian overstepped in the area of personal discipline—interestingly, not *too little*, but *too much*.

Who can argue with a believer who insists Christians should be morally pure? Tatian insisted that we must work to perfect ourselves through harsh physical discipline. Blind to his own spiritual pride, he left the Church to start a strict, legalistic church of his own—known as the "Self-Controlled" or "Masters of Themselves." Its main characteristic was a hatred and fear of "the flesh"—and his followers severed offending hands and cut out lustful eyes.

Though the early fathers taught Christians a balanced respect for the body—because it will be raised and glorified at the resurrection—this was "too weak" for Tatian. Even though his doctrines are, otherwise, purely orthodox, it was *unorthodox practice* that branded him a *heretic*. Christians today who follow unbalanced teachings need to think about Tatian's mistake.

Even so, his writings were circulated—with

warnings—by the early Church fathers. And they can inspire us with boldness when, like Tatian, we are called to witness of Christ to the pagan unbelievers of our day.

Tertullian (ca. A.D. 160–220) also began brilliantly and later fell under a cloud. When he was converted, around A.D. 196, his training as a lawyer helped him to write powerful defenses of the Faith—and the wonderful commentary on "The Lord's Prayer" that is quoted here.

Then came a fresh outpouring of the Holy Spirit. But what began joyfully turned grave when a so-called "new revelation" swept in: *Montanism* forced rigid rules on naive converts. Tertullian became a critic of *grace* and the Church, and his tone changed. Bitterly, he declared: "Jesus said, 'I am the Truth,' not 'I am the custom.' "

So, from good beginnings, Tertullian and Tatian became the fathers of every church that steals the inner-life work of the Holy Spirit through grace and forces believers to "sanctify" themselves by good works.

Clement of Alexandria. (ca. A.D. 153–217) Fortunately, we now come to Clement. This is a man to love!

Picture Clement's world—in which homosexuality was common practice, and immorality paraded in the public baths. To him, the new converts came, barely strong enough in spirit to resist the world's temptations. Picture him, with the fierce protectiveness of a bear, taking in these sin-scarred young men and women. There you have Clement, the pastor and man.

Clement, the bishop, was a truly rare container of that "new life from above." He had traveled widely as a new convert and had absorbed the best spiritual teaching of his day—probably from Ignatius, Polycarp, Justin, and others. Jerome called him "the most learned of the ancients." His works are rich in literary references: Living near one of the greatest libraries of all antiquity no doubt helped. And many have praised Clement for his holy life in the midst of a debauched culture.

Clement loved the Church—those entrusted to his spiritual care. And he loved Christ. Clement was as earthy in his counsels about sexuality as he was sublime in the prayers he offered to the One he knew as "the Living Light."

Theophilus of Antioch (ca. A.D. 115–181) was the spiritual heir of Barnabas and Ignatius, as bishop.

Born a pagan, Theophilus was reading the sacred Scriptures when, all in a moment, the Light of Life rose within him. And he knew Christ. Characteristically, his appeals to the pagans are seasoned with compassion—not so

17

his attacks against some Christian teachers of his day, who were dividing the flock with more heretical "new teachings from the Holy Spirit."

So sensitive is he to perceiving God's invisible but powerful presence that his influence spills down to us through the ages, in the writings of spiritual greats like Augustine and John of the Cross.

Now come three men who are not only alight with wisdom and the flame of new life—they are bonfires! The apostles in heaven must have sighed with relief when the Church was led by Athenagoras, Irenaeus, and Cyprian.

Athenagoras was possibly the head of a Christian school in Alexandria, after Clement's day. Some traditions say that as a youth he'd heard Paul—if so, he was very young. But the dates of Athenagoras' birth and death are uncertain, and his brilliant *Apology* may have been presented to Emperor Marcus Aurelius in A.D. 177, sometime after his death.

His writing is clear and elegant. You will be challenged and inspired by his unflinching belief in the invisible God, who is above all human thought, whose Spirit holds together every created thing. Outworn paganism was fast losing its hold on the world, and the Enemy was in retreat (at least temporarily): Athenagoras gave him the boot as he hobbled off in defeat.

And this Church father captured, as in crystal, the purest Christian spirituality of his day.

Irenaeus. As Marcus Aurelius was in Rome reading the *Apology*, another firebrand was lighting the Way of Christ into greater Europe. Irenaeus became bishop of the next most important city in the Empire—Lyons, in Gaul.

Lying at the head of the Rhône River, Lyons was a hub of culture, trade and commerce, politics—and it was the chief city of an imperial cult. A literal crossroads of the world. Lyons had just martyred one Christian bishop. But if anyone could rise to such a challenge, it was Irenaeus.

A pupil of Justin Martyr, he had possibly heard John teach, and maybe Paul as well. As Justin was led to the block, Irenaeus reached to intercept the falling banner of Christ: It fell to him to drive heretics from the Church, defend against doddering paganism, teach followers the Way of Christ—all of this, in a show-place church.

Still, the purity of his personal devotion was such that he could write, after many years in Christ: "The love of God, being so rich and ungrudging, always gives more than you ask of it." His extraordinary teachings on the resurrection life, which are included here, hold some surprises—and make me chuckle to think I used to fear dying.

Cyprian of Carthage. Pagan Rome's last major attack fell upon Cyprian and other Church leaders in A.D. 249—only months after Cyprian became bishop of this important spiritual center. By Cyprian's own account, so beautiful a Light flooded into him at his conversion, he could never deny the new life he'd experienced.

The persecutions, under Decian and Valerian, were swift and bloody: Christians were scourged to death, burned with irons—and if you think they died begging for their lives, think again.

Read Cyprian's accounts of the martyrs, and you'll witness them at the moment they leap across the border from death to Life with a shout—*"Christ is the Victor!"* In A.D. 258 Cyprian would leave this life, also a martyr, with those same exultant words on his lips.

Not least, but last, the anonymous author of the *Letter to Diognetus* has given us a masterwork of our Faith. Filled with supernatural faith, and a love for humanity, it was written to the tutor of a Roman emperor, about A.D. 256.

The writer reminds us that, for the Christian, "earth is a foreign land. . . . Heaven alone is our fatherland, and our soul's true home."

I owe a great debt to Jaroslav Pelikan, of Yale University. His series *The Christian Tradition: A*

*History of the Development of Doctrine** walked me into the world of these, the apostolic fathers, and opened the heart of their challenging mission to me.

The previous volumes in this series include my suggested prayers with each entry: Not so this one. For many centuries, the voices of these great heroes have not been heard by everyday Christians. I want to leave you alone with them, to let their hearts speak directly to your heart—to let your spirit respond to the inspiration and vision they impart.

And so, I leave you to a wonderful, forty-day journey in the company of these great men of the early Church—men who opened the way to deeper life in Christ for me. In parting, I offer you the same challenges they offered me:

What kind of active, real response does their faithfulness to Christ demand from us? Will the people who come after us—in our families, communities, and our nations—find us as willing to give our all for Christ? If we try to keep the "river of new life" just for ourselves, for our personal, private pleasure, will it always just dry up?

A river will always press on to cut a course. . . . Where will the water of life course as it flows through you?

David Hazard
November 1995

---

*University of Chicago Press

1
The Word, Who Gives Life

A man came up to Jesus and asked, "Teacher, what good thing must I do to get eternal life?"

———

Matthew 19:16

Jesus said, ". . . Whoever eats my flesh and drinks my blood has eternal life. . . . Just as the living Father sent me and I live because of the Father, so the one who feeds on me will live because of me. [I am] the bread that came down from heaven. . . . The Spirit gives life; the flesh counts for nothing. The words I have spoken to you are Spirit and they are life."

———

John 6:54, 57–58, 63

Like you, I once thought I was free. But I was a captive, lying bound in spiritual darkness.

Oh yes, I was free to live just as I pleased. But for a long time, I was empty within. I searched continually for something to believe in. Though I acted confident, inwardly I was tossed like a wave by the wind. I was also drawn to all the things this age boasts in—possessions, power. But in my heart I knew these things were like nothing more than foam on the sea, here now, then bursting and gone forever. Though I was confident outwardly, I was unsure and knew that I was only wandering through life, with no direction, and no sure home for my soul.

As you can see, I knew nothing of real life—the new life that is offered to us from above. Because I was seeking truth through my own experiences, based on my own ways of reasoning, the Truth kept eluding me. And because I relied on my own understanding, the Light of God's real presence was only a distant glimmer.

Then I heard it said that men and women can be "born again"—that God himself had revealed a way for this new birth to take place in us because of His love for wandering creatures like myself.

At first, I thought, *Impossible.*

How could someone like me—with a character as worldly and hardened as mine—change and become as a new creature? How could anyone like me pass beneath the waters and come up declaring I was reborn? It made no sense to me that I would look the same physically, but I would be changed at the core of my being and become like a new man.

I was not quiet about my disbelief—my resistance to this idea of being "born from above."

"We are made of flesh and blood," I objected. "Our drives are natural. Instinctive. Ingrained right into our flesh. It's in our nature to put ourselves first. To dominate and rule and fight to win over others at all cost.

"And then there are habits we've picked up. Even though they may hurt us, these things become as much a part of us as our flesh and bone. How can a person who has loved drinking and feasting become self-controlled and moderate? How can you wake up one morning and gladly dress yourself in simple clothing, when you've always loved fine suits—and all the attention and compliments they bring? How can you live as a humble human being, when you've craved and achieved honor in the public eye?"

I was fully resolved in my position: If you love wine it will always hold you in its grip; the proud man will always be puffed up; anger will always control the man of rage. Cruelty, ambition, lust— these things will never let go of you. . . .

This was my natural way of thinking because I myself was in bondage to countless errors that dwelled in my own flesh. In fact, I despaired of the ability to change. *These habits may be bad for me, but they're a part of me. And since it's impossible to change, why fight it? I might as well indulge myself.*

And then . . .

One day I made a single, simple, necessary step toward God. I humbled myself before Him, and like a child I said, "*I believe.*" I went beneath the blessed waters . . . and inwardly the water of the Spirit cleansed away the grime of my past, as if a stain were removed from fine linen. And something more occurred.

A light fell upon me, as if from above. I was bathed in gentle peace. All at once I was clean. My darkened heart was infused with His presence, and I knew . . . *I knew* . . . that the spiritual barrier between myself and God was gone. Our two hearts were reconciled. Presently, I was aware of the Spirit—the very breath of the Father—coming into me from beyond this world.

And in that moment I was made a new man.

From that time on I have grown in the spiritual knowledge of how to live in a way that nurtures and aids this new life that is given to me. Things I had doubted, I must now treat as Truth and surety. What I'd kept hidden must be brought out into the Light. As a result, what I'd misunderstood about God and the spiritual world began to come clear.

And as for those habits of my old nature—well, I have learned how to change . . . so that this earthly flesh is being remade by God. Each day I continue to grow, as I am made stronger and made alive in the Spirit of holiness. . . .

Now I will tell you, simply, the first step in this way of the Spirit:

Come before God each day, always with holy reverence. Like an innocent child, trust Him.

This attitude will protect your soul. It will keep you from becoming like some, who are so sure they are "saved" that they become careless. For then our old Enemy, who is always lying in wait, takes them captive again.

Begin today to walk in the way of innocence, which is the way of right living before God and man. Walk with a firm step. By that I mean, firmly resolve that you will depend on God with all your heart and strength. . . .

Do you not sense Him, the Father, as He exists all around you? He is willing to flood you. . . . Only go to Him, thirsting for new life. . . . Open your soul now and experience His grace—that is, freedom, love, and power pouring into you from above, filling you to overflowing.

Open your soul to Him now who is your Father and Creator. Be ready to receive and be filled with this new life . . . which is God himself.

Cyprian,
First Epistle

2
Life . . . From Above

We have not stopped praying for you and asking God to fill you with the knowledge of his will through all spiritual wisdom and understanding . . . in order that you may live a life worthy of the Lord . . . and may please him in every way; bearing fruit . . . growing in the knowledge of God . . . strengthened with all power . . . so that you may have great endurance and patience . . . joyfully giving thanks to the Father, who has qualified you to share . . . in the kingdom of light . . . the kingdom of [Jesus], the Son he loves . . . for he is the beginning and the firstborn from among the dead. . . . [And] I have become [a] servant [to you other members of the body of Christ] to present to you . . . the mystery that has been kept hidden for ages. . . .

Colossians 1:9–13, 18, 25–26

---

*I*t is no earthly discovery, this new life that has been given to us. Nor is it a product of human wisdom—something we reasoned out, or conceived

28

in our own minds—this life from above which we are bound to guard so carefully. No, for we have something far better than human mysteries to give out to the world.

Here is the truth we guard carefully and deliver to the dark world:

Our great and mighty Father—He who created the universe and all that is in it, seen and unseen—has sent down from heaven the seed of a new kind of life. So lavish is His love that He is scattering this seed everywhere. The seed is contained in His Word, which forms in us right thinking about God. It trains us, not only in holy thinking, but in right living. His truth does not make "sense" to men whose minds are darkened, because it is higher than our natural minds and it goes against all our low and darkened ways.

And yet, in His love, He broadcasts this seed on the poor soil of our heart—corrupted as it is with fears of loss and death, and with longings for things that can never give us the life we crave. And, by a miracle, His Word takes root. Then, because of His great love, He himself tends this seed by His Spirit, until the root is firm.

We know that this great gift of new life is of highest importance to God. How? Because He did not send a servant—a mere angel—to plant this new life in us. He sent His own Son. Listen to what we are telling you, so no one may lead you astray with their wrong ideas or false teachings. He sent

29

Jesus to reveal to us His true heart—the heart of a loving Father.

For Jesus *is* Lord of this creation. He is the One who, with the Father, both conceived and created the heavens. He set the boundaries of the oceans—and more than that, He governs the mysterious laws that hold all the elements in their delicate balance. He measured the seasons and set the schedule by which the days grow longer or shorter. . . . Yes, all things—in heaven and earth and under the earth, the sea and all that passes within its currents, fire and air, spirits in the heights and depths—He holds the key to their well-being and peace. The Father sent the Son to this, His own now-fallen creation, to announce the gift of new life.

Now the worldly powers impose their government, and their plans, by pressure and the use of terror. But God does not impose His will over us in this way. *Take note of this—for there are already false teachers among us who use fear to manipulate.* No, God came to us as the Son of Man, in gentleness and humility. Indeed, He is the king of all creation—and yet He came as a Savior. By His life and death, He gently persuades us . . . for what kind of God would He be if He had to resort to force?

In Christ, therefore, God *invites* us to share in this new life. He does not argue and threaten.

In Christ, God reveals himself as a lover, showing us all that we might enjoy by learning to live close to Him. At a later time, the Father will indeed send Jesus Christ to be the Judge of all—and no one will be able to ignore His coming, as they do today. But now He does not harass us with constant criticism, pointing out our many flaws and sins.

Consider the witness of those Christians who know Him best: They are so sure of His love for them, and eternal life is already so strong within them, that nothing can make them deny the Lord—not even when they are tortured or thrown to the wild beasts in the arena. No, in fact, every day more and more and more courageous men and women are forsaking this earthly life, which they cannot keep. And by their deaths they demonstrate the power of life eternal, which they cannot lose. As they fall to the earth, they scatter the seed of new life, too. And every day, more are added to the body of Christ, for they see that we have nothing to fear.

Can this be the work of men? Impossible, for it goes against all so-called earthly wisdom. No, the kind of life that rules over all things—even death—this can only come down to us by the power of God. It is the sign that He has come among us . . . and that His new reign among men is now beginning.

LETTER TO DIOGNETUS
(author unknown)

3

We Have Seen Him

In the beginning was the Word, and the Word was with God, and the Word was God. . . . In him was life, and that life was the light of men. . . . No one has ever seen God, but God the only Son, who is at the Father's side, has made him known.

John 1:1, 4, 18

Christ is the exact likeness of the unseen God. . . .

Colossians 1:15, TLB

*W*as there anyone in all humankind who could tell us exactly what God was like before Jesus came?

There are many who came before Christ who had seen glimpses and bright shadows. There were myths and legends, based in man's sense that there is power and wisdom greater than ours. Some have even come claiming to be God—but where are they now?

And then there are the philosophers, of course. Each one argues that his way of reasoning and living is better than anyone else's. But they reason from what they *see*, and not from what is revealed from above. So their reasoning is limited by their human senses as they make assumptions about God that are based on what they can understand from the created world.

For instance, one group of philosophers insists that God is *fire*, since fire has so much destructive power . . . another group claims that water is more powerful . . . and so on, endlessly, through the various elements of nature—wind, lightning, the brutality of beasts. Each one insists their god is more powerful than all the others. And each group misses the point: Why should any created thing be superior to another—since each one has some force that can conquer it?

So the wisdom of the world is mostly speculation and guesswork. Sometimes it is deception, held out to wandering souls by those who crave power over others.

But now God has come, in the flesh, to reveal himself to us—that is, His true nature. And the world does not recognize God in Jesus, because it has not seen Him or understood Him. The world only understands power and brutishness. The world understands rulers who demand respect, honor, and obedience from those they hold in subjection by force. The world only understands what it sees.

And what we see—with the spiritual light of God's truth as He has revealed it—is a creation that has fallen into disorder. So that one creature lives off another, and fear governs. And the panicked struggle to resist and to survive controls all flesh.

Therefore, God had to reveal himself by *faith*— for faith is the way the soul sees, and it is only by faith that we can see God. For God is nothing like His creatures. The means by which He rules creation is not like earthly, visible powers.

God, the One who made all things and placed them in their proper order, governs with the patient love of a good father. Not that He merely loves men and women—no, all His actions are compelled by His tender compassion for us. Toward us, He is gentle, He is calm, He is always true.

He always was, and always is, and always will be the outpouring of goodness. For as Jesus revealed, *the Father is goodness itself.*

Open the eyes of your soul, then, and in faith behold Him: He is Goodness. Then you will know Him as He is.

Long ago, the Father revealed this "secret" of His nature to the Son. . . . And now, in Christ, He has removed the veil that covered our spiritual eyes—that is, ignorance, fear, and unbelief, and our blind wandering after lesser gods. He has shown us everything that He prepared for us from the beginning, before our sad fall. Now, too, He gives

us everything we need to walk in this new life—
spiritual gifts, empowering grace. . . .

For long ages past, He allowed us to wander
lost in our sins and brutishness. By this, He proved
that in our mortal nature we are not able to obtain
the inner life we crave. . . . Now, He wants us to live
in spirit by believing fully in His goodness; He
wants us to come to Him, seeing Him as our only
father, guardian, teacher, counselor, physician. He
wants His goodness to fill and form our every
thought and to light our way through this crooked
and dark world that is anything but good.

As you meditate on His goodness, it will indeed
fill you—it will become your honor, your glory,
your strength. Goodness will become life to your
soul!

Our faith is not based, then, on the speculations
of men. It is based on the goodness of God revealed
in Christ Jesus. And it is the kind of faith you can
have—making you strong against all the onslaughts
of the world. This faith is freely yours. If only you
want it, if only you receive it.

LETTER TO DIOGNETUS

4
First Principles of Faith

By faith we understand that the universe was formed at God's command, so that what is seen was not made out of what was visible.

Hebrews 11:3

*I*t is important for you to understand the difference between *faith* and *reason*. For some believers confuse the two, and as a result, they lose their way. . . .

Human reason is the process by which we gain knowledge about this physical world in which we live for now. As we experiment we understand causes and effects, and we reason out the ways that this created world works.

This type of reasoning knowledge is wholly dependent upon our senses—that is, our abilities to see, feel, hear, touch, and taste. Through sensing we are led to reasoning and understanding. From understanding, to knowledge. And then we form our opinions.

But far above this way of knowing are the first principles of our knowledge—the knowledge of God, given to us by revelation. For the principles of our faith were revealed to us by God, from above, by the Spirit. These principles cannot be demonstrated in the same way that we can observe the basic laws that govern our physical world. . . .

Human knowledge, then, is a state of mind that results from amassing physical evidence and from seeing how things work.

But *faith* is a grace—the light of God, poured out within us. Faith accepts truths that cannot be "proved." Faith comprehends the simplest truths, which invisibly govern and hold together the whole universe—even though these truths can never be demonstrated to the satisfaction of our senses, dependent as they are on observing the material world. For the Truth of God is spiritual and pure, and lies above all that is created and fallen.

. . . Spiritual faith does not come about by saying, "Show me a sign, God. Answer my prayer. Perform a miracle." It begins by believing simply that *God is*—and He is above His creation.

"Behold, I make new things," says the Word, "which eye has not seen, and ear has not heard, nor has it entered into the heart of man" (1 Corinthians 2:9; Isaiah 64:4).

Ask God, therefore, to give you a new eye, a new ear, and a new heart. For whatever your human senses insist that you believe *must* be brought under the spirit. Otherwise you will always be under the dominion and control of the flesh and of the world. You will always interpret the events of your life by what your senses tell you, and not by the Light of faith.

The disciple of the Lord must train himself to see, hear, speak, and act spiritually. Therefore, we do not insist that God answer prayers, or bless us, in order to "prove" He is Lord. That is fleshly-minded darkness, and a counterfeit form of our faith.

Learn how to walk in the true faith—which rests in God, not demanding earthly answers and blessings. Do not slip down into a false, earthly faith, which must rest upon answers, signs, and miracles in order to stand at all.

Clement of Alexandria,
MISCELLANEOUS TEACHINGS

5
Our Kingdom Is Above

*T*he LORD *has established his throne in heaven, and
his kingdom rules over all.*

———

Psalm 103:19

*J*esus [said], *"The kingdom of God does not come
visibly. . . ."*

———

Luke 17:20

*S*ince earliest times men have seen the earth and sky and
all God made, and have known of his existence and great
eternal power. Instead of worshiping the glorious, ever-
living God, they took wood and stone and made idols for
themselves. . . .

———

Romans 1:20, 23, TLB

We Christians have been criticized and hated for not worshiping and living as you pagans do. And that is because we do not pay homage at your temples, offering sacrifices and draping flower garlands around the statues of your so-called gods. (Nor do we abandon our children outside our homes, as is your custom, to be picked up by your pagan priests for their degrading and horrible practices in your temples.)

We know the truth about your temples and your "gods." Your statues are dead. They do not represent the likeness of God at all. For we do know that the one true God does not possess a form like anything our minds can imagine. Rather, your statues are fashioned in the shapes in which demons appeared to your men of old. For your forefathers were tricked and cowed, through fear, into believing that the fallen angels were gods.

Let us be honest and reasonable. How can you believe there is any power in statues and objects of nature that were shaped by your own craftsmen? They are chiseled from rock. Or cut and scraped from wood. Or poured as molten metal into molds and then beaten into shape with hammers. Oh yes, these are powerful gods you worship! . . .

And now, the demons who hide behind the mask of your gods promise you secret powers, and also spread lies about us. . . .

For instance, you have heard that we are watching and waiting for a new kingdom to come. In your earthly way of thinking, you jump to the wrong conclusion. You think we are planning to seize political power and set up a kingdom here and now. Nothing is further from the truth.

When we speak of our kingdom, we mean the spiritual Kingdom of God. This kingdom is in our hearts, where Christ rules as our Lord. He commands our full allegiance, in body and soul, so that we put no created thing before Him—not even our own lives.

Surely what I'm saying must be obvious to you. For when you haul us into your courts and put us on trial for treason against your government, what do we say? We say that Christ is our Lord and King, that His invisible Kingdom is our true fatherland—even though the penalty for confessing this is death. If we were planning to establish an earthly kingdom, why would we think it an honor to give away our lives? Wouldn't we be sneaking around, or in hiding, planning a violent takeover?

Our refusal to worship created things, and our refusal to cling to our lives, points to one fact about us as Christians: We do not place our hopes in the present creation, for it is fallen and is passing way. And we are at peace about death—for we are all going to die anyway.

Now I must speak the truth about you.

It is odd to me that you distrust and hate Christians so much. For, in fact, we are the best citizens in your empire when it comes to living orderly, peaceable lives—and we even pay the outrageous taxes you demand. . . . Though we have no hope in this world order, we live good lives here because we believe our rewards or punishments await us in the Kingdom of our Father. He sees all things, and His judgments are eternal. So we aim to live virtuous lives now while you—I must speak the truth—you conceal your evil actions, then hypocritically pretend you are good people when you appear in public.

... If you must continue to live like thoughtless creatures—even though you pride yourself in your mental abilities and philosophies and literature—then so be it. If you prefer your old way of living to the truth, that is your choice.

Do what you must to us. ... But the Word has declared that neither you nor your gods will win in the end.

Justin Martyr,
FIRST APOLOGY
(To the Emperor)

6

"Luxury Has Deranged Us"

It is God's will that you should be holy; that you should avoid sexual immorality; that each of you should learn to control his own body in a way that is holy and honorable, not in passionate lust like the heathen, who do not know God. . . .

1 Thessalonians 4:3–5

For although they knew God, they neither glorified him as God nor gave thanks to him, but their thinking became futile and their foolish hearts were darkened. . . . Therefore, God gave them over in the sinful desires of their hearts to sexual impurity for the degrading of their bodies with one another.

Romans 1:21, 24

I am writing this strict warning to you who are followers of the Way and of Christ.

You must in no way take on the customs of the worldly people around you. Under the guise of physical conditioning, they, in fact, worship and glory in their own bodies.

Consider the men of our generation and how they behave in the gymnasium. They spend much time preening themselves, even plucking the hair so they become smooth. Some do this to attract other men, in the manner of women. Others primp and smooth in order to attract women—even though they have wives at home—and so they become adulterers.

Keep your distance from people like this. For they will try to convince you there is nothing wrong with "taking care of your body," or "making yourself look good," or being "attractive." In fact, they want to justify their own sins against the body by convincing you to act just like them. . . .

I shrink from even mentioning the evil practices that are carried on in the public baths and in the gymnasium. And it horrifies me to think of the young people who go to such places for normal, good, and healthy reasons, only to be enticed and corrupted by those who lie in wait for such innocence—there where the very prowess of our human body can be tried by sport and honored for its God-given strength. Instead, the most unnatural practices are carried on. Isn't this the height of perversion?

More and more men are becoming bold in this shameful way. They are not the least embarrassed

44

to engage in perversions in public. What would they not do in private?—"What we do in our own homes is our business!" they insist.

But among us, the man who would be "attractive" should clothe and care for the most beautiful thing in him—his mind. Every day he should be growing in those good qualities that honor a man. Instead of plucking out hairs, as the heathen do, be man enough to pluck out *lust*. . . .

It is sad—no, it is disgusting—to think that men today openly practice things which normal men would rather die than do. But life has reached a fever-pitch of lust . . . and evil, unbridled sexuality permeates our towns and cities. . . . Women offer their flesh for hire. Boys dress like women and offer themselves to men.

I will tell you the truth: Luxury has deranged us. . . . Because we crave pleasure, we have turned from God and the Way of Life. And when above all else, you seek luxury and the niceties of life, then you will be driven by lust to try everything. Lust is like fire; it knows no bounds. But the more things you try, the sooner you become bored. And lust, which is unquenchable, forces you to try anything—even that which is unnatural. Until you yourself are corrupted. . . .

I cry to God in agony of spirit because of the wickedness that is destroying so many. . . .

I approve of the simplicity of the barbarians who follow Christ—far more than the luxury of our sophisticated culture, which is destroying us.

Loving the life that is not weighed down by fine things, the barbarians have seen through the vanity of luxuries.

This is how the Lord wants us to be: Stripped and free of luxury—stripped in spirit of the vain thinking that you cannot live without luxury. Take with you only the bare wood of life. Then your only aim will be to work out your salvation.

Clement of Alexandria,
THE INSTRUCTIONS

7
Our Choice

*Now what I am commanding you today is not too
difficult for you or beyond your reach. . . . See, I set
before you today life and prosperity, death and
destruction. For I command you today to love the LORD
your God, to walk in his ways, and to keep his
commands, decrees and laws; then you will live and
increase, and the LORD your God will bless you. . . .*

Deuteronomy 30:11, 15–16

*T*he prophetic Spirit speaks to us of things that
are to come—and He speaks with certainty, as if
they have already happened.

David spoke of the coming of Christ, for
example, and of His suffering and death. (See
Psalm 22.) These prophecies were given more than
fifteen hundred years *before* Christ! . . . And more
recently, what has been shown us by the prophetic
Spirit through the apostles makes us look forward
with certainty and excitement to the incorruptible
eternal life that lies ahead of us.

And yet there is a matter of some confusion

among you. Some are teaching that because an event is foreknown to God and predicted to us, every event yet to come is inevitable. They claim that we believe in destiny, or fate, in the same way that the pagans speak of fate. This is untrue.

Specifically, we have heard from the prophets that punishments and rewards will be given to each man and woman according to their actions. If these rewards and punishments were already fixed by fate, nothing would be left to our will and choosing. And if one person is fated to be good and another evil, no one's actions are good or bad. If the human race has not been given the power of choice and free will—to avoid shameful behavior and embrace what is good—then we are not responsible for our actions.

Isn't the struggle between good and evil in your own soul enough evidence that such thinking is nonsense? Each one of us depends on the strength of the Spirit to walk uprightly with God and man— or we choose to pursue temptation and fall under the power of sin. And make no mistake, what we do is always a matter of our own free choice.

Consider, I say, your own spiritual struggles when temptation falls upon you. Are you not pulled, sometimes this way and sometimes that way—torn by opposing desires? If you were fated to be good or evil, why would you struggle at all? You would not be able to go back and forth in your mind, thinking:

Yes, I'll go ahead and do this thing . . . it won't matter, and God will forgive me.

Or, *No, this thing is wrong and goes against God.*

The pagans, of course, fail to understand why we would resist "natural desires" at all. They say there is no such thing as "virtue" or "vice." They say that right and wrong is only a matter of opinion. The higher wisdom that comes from above—from the One who is Reason itself—shows us that such thinking proceeds from the lower reasoning abilities of man. Mostly, man's reasoning is an attempt to justify our impiety and wickedness.

What we teach is this: Those who choose to live good lives can fully expect well-deserved rewards from the Lord in eternity—and in that sense, they are *destined*. Likewise, those who choose evil are *destined* for punishment—and this is of their own choosing because they have been forewarned and have mocked the warning.

Let's be clear that our teaching springs from a different starting point, a different source, than the beliefs of the pagans. For they believe that man is just the same as animals and trees, with no real power to choose. We know that God has made man of a higher order, and the power to choose is his.

So God does know ahead of time what men and women will do with their lives. He decrees that they will be rewarded—that is, He will do to us according to what we have done. This gives us a different view of the prophetic Spirit.

For God is always speaking to the human race,

warning us, guiding us. By His Spirit, He causes us to reflect on our choices, remembering that one day we must answer to someone who is higher and wiser than ourselves.

Learn to see His warnings, then, as one way He shows His care for us. For His laws and warnings are not meant to grieve and burden us. The Spirit of prophecy is one way He guides us into lives that are safe from the ruin of evil—lives that are peaceful, happy, and free.

By this, I think you can see that there is no room for "fate" or "destiny," as the unenlightened pagan philosophers think.

Justin Martyr,
First Apology

8

The World's Unreasoning Hatred

[Jesus said,] "Remember the words I spoke to you: 'No servant is greater than his master.' If they persecuted me, they will persecute you also . . . this is to fulfill what is written. . . . 'They hated me without reason.'"

John 15:20, 25

In fact, everyone who wants to live a godly life in Christ Jesus will be persecuted, while evil men and impostors will go from bad to worse, deceiving and being deceived.

2 Timothy 3:12–13

There was a certain woman whose husband made no secret of his adulterous affairs. Before this woman was a Christian, she too had slept with many other men.

As she learned the teachings of Christ Jesus, she understood the spiritual freedom that comes as we learn to control the lusts and demands of the flesh. She tried to explain these things to her husband, hoping that he too might be set free from his lustful way of life. Patiently, carefully, she explained the Light of Christ that has come to shine on our hearts with holy reason. She told him of the eternal fire that awaits those whose souls become seared and deadened to God's true and pure love because they have been burned over by the fires of lust.

He ignored her, though, and continued in his lustful lifestyle. Valuing his own pleasure more than her pleas, he soon killed her affection for him. In fact, his sexual pursuits had become wilder, and he engaged in acts that go against nature and everything that is right and decent.

At first, she considered divorcing him. . . . Then close friends convinced her she ought to stay with her husband so that, perhaps, by her right living and her prayers she might win him to Christ. So she forced herself to stay.

Then he made a business trip to a major city. Soon she heard reports that his conduct was more outrageous than ever. She could no longer stay joined to him, sharing his table and his bed. And so she presented him with a bill of divorce and left.

You would think this man would have been shocked into seeing how wretched his behavior had made him. You would think he would see how much better his wife's life had become since she gave up carousing at drunken parties, not to mention the reckless sexual exploits of her past life. You would think that his heart would be touched by her tender, patient concern for him—and by her heartfelt pleas that he save his sexual passions only for her, and she for him.

Instead, his pride was wounded. To think that she would leave him, when he wanted a wife to come home to and use at will!

And so, O Emperor, this man presented you with a petition. He asked that you prosecute his wife—solely on the grounds that she is a "Christian."

This woman also petitioned you, begging that she be allowed to put her household in order before you drag her into your courts and, most likely, into prison.

When the husband could not satisfy his rage at her immediately, he brought a charge against the man who had taught her to be a Christian. . . . This man was placed in chains and abused for a long time, just for being a Christian. . . . Eventually, he was executed.

When a second Christian man protested this unjust treatment, he too was executed. (And as he was being led to the execution, he shouted, "Thank you, Father, that I am being freed from such evil rulers. I come to you now, O King of Heaven.")

A third Christian man also protested—and he was arrested and sent to the torturer. . . !

This is my question to you, Emperor:

Are you a lover of wisdom—or are you only a lover of men's opinions so that you will be popular and well-liked? And what good is it to be praised by men if their lives and words are false and abusive? While you respect the words of such evil-hearted men just because they bend the knee to you, you punish us though we speak the simple truth and do not falsely accuse.

What would you say to your own Socrates, who has declared, "No man must be honored before truth"?

Justin Martyr,
SECOND APOLOGY
(To the Roman Senate)

9
On Nature Worship

*T*his is what the LORD says, ". . . I am the first and I am the last; apart from me there is no God. . . . All who make idols are nothing, and the things they treasure are worthless. . . . [The heathen idols] know nothing, they understand nothing; their eyes are plastered over so they cannot see, and their minds closed so they cannot understand. . . . Remember these things . . . for I have made you, you are my servant."

Isaiah 44:6, 9, 18, 21

[*H*ear the word of the Lord,] "I don't want your sacrifices—I want your love; I don't want your offerings—I want you to know me."

Hosea 6:6, TLB

*M*en of Greece, why are you stirring up the authorities to attack us so viciously? Why are you trying to convince them we are criminals?

When the sovereign orders us to pay tribute, we pay. When a Christian is ordered by his master to work hard, as bondsmen are obliged to do, we work without complaining.

You would have us persecuted because of a philosophical difference, even though we have committed no crime. The difference between us is this: We believe that God is the only one who deserves complete respect, full trust, and worship—while men are to be honored as men, not gods. When you ask us to obey some civil law or a decree of the sovereign that goes against God, of course we cannot do that. This is what makes you furious.

And now you command me to submit to your pagan laws and customs and worship—you command me to deny God himself—and I cannot. I might as well be clear: I will never obey you in this matter. I would rather die than betray my God or show myself ungrateful for His love.

Why do we so steadfastly refuse to worship your gods as if they are equal to ours? I will tell you about our God, whom you hate and resist.

Unlike your gods, our God has no beginning, and He exists outside of time and its limitations. Our God is the beginning of all things.

Our God is Spirit. He is not contained in matter—such as wood, stone, water, or heavenly bodies—as if such natural things have some life in themselves, as you claim. He is the maker of all spirits, and the one who created matter out of nothing.

He cannot be seen or touched, though He is the Father of all that our eyes can see and our senses feel. He is above His creation—though nature is a window through which we can understand something of His invisible attributes, such as His might and the intricate working of His wisdom.

Now I ask you, how can I worship a thing, a mere object—like one of your statues, or one of your so-called sacred places in nature? Your statues were created by men—do you hear what I am saying to you?—they did not even have the power to resist the sculptor's hammer and chisel. They lie there docile and subservient to the imagination and skill and tools of mortal men! How can I worship and adore objects that are meant for my service and have even less power in themselves than I do? How can wood and stone *contain* gods, or *be* gods?

Yes, we teach that there is a power by which the Spirit of God holds together even the elements (see Colossians 1:15–17)—and so in this sense the Spirit of God pervades matter. (It is this that you perceive in nature and make the mistake of thinking it has power in itself to help you.) But matter is of a lower order, and we do not teach that it has life in it or power to give. Certainly, nothing inanimate can contain the Holy Spirit. And even when the Holy Spirit comes to dwell in the soul of a Christian, giving us new life from above, we are in no way to be honored as if we were equals of God. He alone is perfect.

We do not even teach that Christians must present material gifts to God. (Our gifts to the church are for the benefit of others here on earth.) For He who is high above all things needs nothing of ours. So we do not tell our people, "God needs your gifts." To represent Him as if He were some poor beggar in the streets is unthinkable to us.

What we teach, simply, is this: God is the necessary ground of all that exists. From Him all things spring, whether visible or invisible. In Him, all things have their existence . . . and all power is His . . . and nothing is His equal. . . .

Tatian,
ADDRESS TO THE
GREEKS

10
Wolves

*[J*esus said,] ". . . many false prophets will appear and
deceive many people."

Matthew 24:11

I am astonished that you are so quickly deserting the
one who called you by the grace of Christ and are
turning to a different gospel—which is really
no gospel at all. . . .

Galatians 1:6–7

---

*F*rom Miletus, Paul sent to Ephesus for the elders of
the church [and] he said to them, ". . . I know that . . .
savage wolves will come in among you. . . . Even from
your own number men will arise and distort the truth
in order to draw away disciples after them. So be on
your guard! . . . Now I commit you to God and to the
word of his grace, which can build you up and give you
an inheritance among all those who are sanctified."

Acts 20:17, 29–32

*S*uppose the apostles had not left us their writings. Would we not let ourselves be ruled in spirit by the tradition they handed down to faithful men, to whom they committed the churches?

Consider the heathen, after all. There are many former pagans, now believers, who live under the rule of Christ, though they have no written Scriptures. What they have is the witness of the Spirit in their hearts, convincing them that the new life and the salvation they longed for have come to us in Christ Jesus.

Hold fast to our tradition, and do not let anyone add to the truth or take away from it with so-called "new teachings" or "new revelations."

For the apostles taught us this:

To believe in one God, the maker of heaven and earth and all that is contained in them. To comprehend God through the appearance of Jesus Christ, the Son of God. To believe that God loved us so greatly He sent His only Son to be born of a virgin. By the power of His Spirit, He accomplished an act that no other being in all creation could do, joining God to man. After that, Jesus suffered under Pontius Pilate; He rose from the dead and was received up into the glories of heaven. From His exalted place on high, He will return to earth—the Savior of those who are saved, and the Judge of those who are to be judged, He will send into eternal fire those who change the truth to suit their own purposes; also those who despise the fact that we owe all obedience to the heavenly Father, and those who deny that He is come into this world in the flesh.

As I've said, there are many who speak barbarian languages and who have never read the Scriptures. Yet they have believed our witness. As a result, their lives have changed drastically. Not only that, but the inward state of their hearts is pure toward God, like innocent children, making their words and lives sweet in right living, in purity, and in simple wisdom. If anyone preached to them the "new teachings" and "revelations" of the heretics who have come among us, they would plug their ears and run away from such lies—so powerful is the old tradition, passed down by word of mouth from the apostles.

And now we see the pure message of God corrupted by many who, in their evil desire to have men submit to them, pervert the truth, claiming God has shown them something new. They add to the simple teaching about life in Christ. I am speaking of Valentinus . . . Marcion . . . and Cerdon. . . . As we have told you elsewhere, these men, and others who are called Gnostics, began with Menander. And Menander was a follower of the first heretic, Simon, once known as "the magician" (see Acts 8:9–24), who was cursed by the apostles for trying to buy the power of the Spirit. Each one of these men rebelled against the Word of God, which commands every man to submit to the Father in the attitude of Christ Jesus. . . .

Be on guard always for the wolves among us—

these men who tear apart the Church so that they can boast in a following of their own. Be on guard, I say, but do not lose heart about the power of the gospel—for the true teaching of the apostles stands. And it will always stand throughout all time, preserved by men and women of the Faith, through the Church. . . .

Let us keep to the first, simple teaching of the apostles, then. . . . For they have demonstrated by their lives that our Lord Jesus Christ *is* the Truth— the only Truth—and in Him there is no lie. . . .

Irenaeus,
AGAINST THE HERESIES

11
The Full Counsel
of Gospel

The counsel of the LORD *standeth forever. . . .*

Psalm 33:11, KJV

[Paul said,] ". . . I have not shunned to declare unto
you all the counsel of God."

Acts 20:27, KJV

It is by God's design that there are four
Gospels. . . .

For the Word, who is the maker and designer of
all things—the One who gave us the fourfold
Gospels—sits enthroned among the cherubim. As
David prayed when he asked about the King who
was to come, "You who sit among the cherubim,
show yourself—shine forth!" (Psalm 80:1).

Why am I making a point to tell you this? For
this reason.

We know that the cherubim are creatures who have four faces, and each face shows us one aspect of the work of the Son of God, our Lord. The first face is like that of a lion, which tells us of the princely work of Christ, who comes to rule the nations. The second face is like that of an ox, telling us of His work as our high priest—and reminding us that He himself is our sacrifice! The third face is like that of a man, speaking of His coming—when He took on our humanity in His compassion for us in our fallen state. The fourth face is like that of an eagle, telling us that Spirit is flown forth from the Father and broods protectively over His people, the Church. . . .

Since the Lord was so careful and loving to give us the four forms of the gospel, let us take care! Do not be foolish or arrogant, like some who have tried to come into the Church. Do not destroy the full counsel of the gospel by teaching only the part of it that you like—say, the part about Christ's sacrificial death for our sins—while ignoring the fact that He is our ruling King.

As we have warned you before, stay away from the heretics and apostates. For they continue to teach that they have been given special and secret knowledge from God—and that these new teachings replace the teaching of Christ. . . .

Likewise, be careful about those who frustrate the Holy Spirit, who has been poured out in these days for the whole human race as the Father has willed. For these men accept many of our doctrines, but they reject John's Gospel altogether, in which Jesus promised to send the Spirit. These men say they are Christians, but they refuse to admit that the Holy Spirit is alive and at work among us today, speaking and guiding us in the Way. . . . These men might as well reject the Apostle Paul, too. For in his first letter to the Corinthians he speaks clearly about the Spirit and the gifts. . . .

Avoid such men, for they sin against the Spirit of God. And if they do not turn from their unbelief, they are in danger of falling into the sin that cannot be forgiven.

Irenaeus,
AGAINST THE HERESIES

12
The Invisible God

*This is what the LORD says: "Heaven is my throne
and the earth is my footstool. Where is the house you
will build for me? Where will my resting place be? . . .
This is the one I esteem: he who is humble and contrite
in spirit, and trembles at my word. But whoever
[thoughtlessly offers] a bull . . . a lamb . . . a grain
offering . . . and burns memorial incense [is] like one
who worships an idol."*

Isaiah 66:1–3

Dear children, keep yourselves from idols.

1 John 5:21

Why do you Greeks insist on turning the
authorities against us so that we must live under
constant, vicious attack? Why are we Christians
hounded and prosecuted like criminals?

If the king orders us to pay even the most
exorbitant taxes, we pay them. When a Christian
bondsman is ordered by his master to work hard,

he serves without complaint. Like good citizens, we honor our authorities and masters.

Only on this point do we differ: God alone deserves our reverent obedience, above all. We fear to displease Him in any way, far more than we fear your threats when we refuse to obey laws and orders that go against the Word of our God. This is what infuriates you, and stirs you up to cause trouble for us.

I tell you plainly, without hesitation—I will never deny God, even though that is what you ask me to do in order to "prove" my allegiance to your government. I would rather die than betray Him who loved me. That would be utmost ingratitude toward the One who gave His life for me.

Here is the true difference between us: You worship gods who your poets and philosophers and myth-makers imagined as they tried to comprehend what divinity must be like. And so you worship gods you created out of your own reasoning. What we know of God did not come to us from our reasoning—God revealed himself to us, in His own way and in His own time.

Further, our God did not begin *in time*. Your gods did. Our God alone is without beginning— and in fact, He is the beginning of all things.

Even more, our God is Spirit. Though there is a certain power of God that holds all things together—even inanimate objects like wood, water, and stone—yet the living Holy Spirit of God does not suffuse gross matter. Yes, He is the maker of all living spirits and all forms of life. But the power by which He holds all the universe together is something less than the living Spirit, who comes to dwell in men who receive Him. And even then, we do not consider any Christian in whom God dwells as equal with God. He cannot be seen or touched—except by *faith*, which comes as God opens our spiritual perception—because all natural men live in gross, fallen flesh.

You, on the other hand, worship what you make with your own hands! We refuse to bow down and beg favors from senseless blocks of stone, wood, and metal. Why would you do such a thing, when you know full well your own craftsmen built these lifeless forms with their own muscle and sweat and imagination? All this I find unbelievable in a nation of reasoning men!

For God has revealed to us the right order of things, which you refuse to accept. All creation is like a window, revealing to us by its qualities something of the virtues and character of God. We are taught that nature—even the sun and moon—were created for man, and we were not created to worship and serve them. How can you ask us to bow down to our own servants?

Finally, you ask us to present gifts and offerings in your temples and to your idols. But we teach that the One who is invisible does not *need* anything from us. The gifts we offer in our churches are distributed among fellow men—widows, orphans, families in need. No Christian would speak of God as if He were a hungry beggar, pleading for our money and belongings. That is unthinkable.

For our God requires nothing . . . except our open hearts . . . and our full allegiance. . . .

Tertian,
ADDRESS TO THE
GREEKS

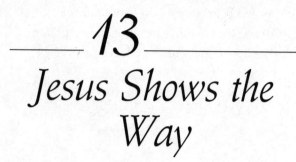

13
Jesus Shows the Way

[He is] perfect in beauty . . .

Psalm 50:2

. . . King of kings and Lord of lords.

Revelation 19:16

. . . A great high priest who has gone through the heavens . . .

Hebrews 4:14

Our Savior, Jesus Christ, far surpasses any of the sons of men, though He was man.

He is the loveliness of divine royalty. And He alone is loved by those whose hearts hunger for true Beauty.

By that I mean He possesses a rare spiritual

attractiveness that those who lust for objects of physical beauty cannot even grasp. But we know He *is* Beauty—the living Light, the One who gives light to every man. (See John 1:9.)

This Jesus has also shown himself to be King of all who live. And He did this in a way no earthly king would—through the wonder of His downcast majesty. Even innocent little children, when they are told He came down from heaven to die on the cross, recognize that He is King of Holiness. . . . And the prophets, speaking forth the words of God, heralded the coming of this King of Beauty.

So rich is He that He merely scoffed when Satan offered Him all the gold in the world along with the glory of men that such wealth would bring. (See Luke 4:1–12.)

And I do not need to tell you that Jesus is a royal priest. And He stands alone before God, possessing the one means by which we may come freely before God to be pardoned of our sins . . . and to find spiritual strength that will help us in our need. (See Hebrews 4:15–16.)

Most important, He did not merely tell us about the Way of Life—as One speaking from on high. He came down to live among us, and He shows us the Way.

Clement of Alexandria,
MISCELLANEOUS TEACHINGS

14
Taught, Like Children

[God himself] will teach us his ways, so that we may walk in his paths.

—

Micah 4:2

For those God foreknew he also predestined to be conformed to the likeness of his Son, that he might be the firstborn among many brothers.

—

Romans 8:29

There is no way we could have learned the ways of God unless our Teacher, the Word, had been made man. For no one else could have shown us what the Father is like, or how He wants us to live—no one except the Word of the Father. He alone knows the mind of God and understands the wisdom of His ways.

Do not be misled: We can learn of God in no

other way than to examine and imitate the life of Jesus. He is our only Teacher.

We begin by imitating Him in His complete childlike submission and obedience to the Father. We make it our practice to become doers of His words—not merely thinking right thoughts about God, but beginning to act on His directives to us. As we act on what He tells us, we understand from within how God wants us to live.

This is how we become one with Him in spirit, thought, and action; then we have true communion. It is then we receive strength and new life within ourselves—life that is not *of* ourselves—from the One who is perfect and before all creation.

(I warn you, there are those who mentally agree with the Scriptures and the teachings of our Lord, but this is not what we mean by following Christ.)

Follow the Way of Life, then, imitating Christ. Do not resist, or think you can come up with another way to God, forgetting what you know. For you are like spiritual babies, just newly reborn by the power of Him who is highest and best. Do not become proud in yourselves, for there is nothing in us worthy of this gift of incorruptible new life—it is purely a gift!

We must remain in this Spirit of Christ if we want to continue to receive life from God. And as we grow He is remaking us in the image of the "new man," Christ Jesus. The Father has always planned for us to grow in the spiritual image of His Son.

This should make your hearts leap. For this world we live in, and these bodies, are destined to pass away because of the curse. But we who are the first to experience new birth—*we are the beginning of His brand-new creation . . . the first sign that He will fulfill His promise to renew the earth. . . .*

Irenaeus,
AGAINST THE HERESIES

15
Our Work Among Angels

*Because you are sons, God sent the Spirit of his Son
into our hearts, the Spirit who calls out, "Abba,
Father."*

Galatians 4:6

*Jesus [said], "The people of this age marry and are
given in marriage. But those who are considered worthy
of taking part in that age [that is to come] and in the
resurrection from the dead will neither marry nor be
given in marriage, and they can no longer die; for they
are like the angels. They are God's children, since
they are children of the resurrection."*

Luke 20:34–36

When we pray in the words of our Lord we
say, "Our Father in heaven, hallowed is your
name. . . ." By that we mean that the name of the

Father is set apart from every other name, to be revered and adored above all others.

Of course it is fitting that we should speak well of God at all times, in every circumstance. We should not be like the unbelieving, doubting His goodness. Instead we should fix in our thoughts all that He has done for our benefit, and by speaking well of God we build ourselves up in the Faith. And faith is what we need to enter and to keep walking in the kingdom of God.

That is the main point I am trying to teach you here. For some mistakenly think that God *needs* to hear our praises—as if He were some earthly king who needs the kind words of His subjects. This is not so. God's name *is* hallowed, and it is we who need to be reminded. For God is not made holy by us, or by our words—we are made holy in Him.

Even the angels who stand nearest the throne of God cry out day and night, in endless awe, as they search the wonders of His being—*"Holy, holy, holy!"* (See Revelation 4:8.) It is the cry of unending delight and amazement.

One day, if we continue to follow the way of salvation, we are destined to step through death into eternal life. And there we will become like the angels. So it is fitting that we begin to practice the greeting that our Father's heavenly children use. Fitting that we should begin to serve Him now as witnesses to all as we learn to say, "Consider the heavenly Father—His name alone is set aside for worship."

So we can begin to do the work of angels now, announcing the glory that comes—and is to come more greatly—into this dark world.

Tertullian,
ON THE PRAYER

16

Strong in "Body"

*W*hat causes fights and quarrels among you? . . .
Submit yourselves . . . to God. Resist the devil, and he
will flee from you [and from your midst]. Come near to
God and he will come near to you . . . Brothers, do not
slander one another. Anyone who speaks against his
brother . . . speaks against the law [of Love]. . . .

James 4:1, 7, 8, 11
[editor's notes]

*B*e eager to come together often in the Lord's
name. When you do so, spend all your time giving
thanks and glory to God.

In this simple way, the powers of Satan are
destroyed. All his efforts to wound you as you walk
the way of Life will be thwarted. For focusing on
the Lord draws you into one accord, which
destroys Satan's efforts to tear apart the body of
Christ through useless disagreements. (When you
spend all your time together arguing, you are
doomed to defeat.) Likewise, when you hear
witness of the clear, pure faith of others, you

yourself are encouraged to greater personal faith in the Lord—so Satan's attempts to separate you from God through fear and doubt are annihilated as well.

You will not fail to notice how spiritual fellowship builds your soul—not if you want to grow more perfect in your faith and love toward Jesus Christ. Faith . . . love . . . these are like fountains of life to our souls.

We begin with faith in God; that is good. And faith in God ends in love toward one another. When these two exist hand in hand, God is there among you. And everything that comes from His outpouring goodness is the result.

Those who profess to be of Christ will always be identified by what they do. For our faith is not like that of the heathen, or the unbelieving. We profess our faith with our mouths—but let us not speak empty words. Let us believe with our hearts and carry through by acting in love.

Love, then, will always be the end result of faith.

Ignatius of Antioch,
LETTER TO THE
EPHESIANS

17
The Deep Mysteries of God

When the time had fully come, God sent his Son, born of a woman, born under the law [of sin and death], to redeem those under the law, that we might receive the full rights of sons.

Galatians 4:4–5
[editor's note]

God has chosen to make known among the Gentiles the glorious riches of this mystery, which is Christ in you, the hope of glory.

Colossians 1:27

When the Virgin was overshadowed by God, and later when she began to labor to give birth, both events escaped the notice of the prince of this age . . . at least for a time.

Consider the manner in which Christ was announced to this age:

A star shone forth from heaven, brighter than all the stars, and its light came as it were from beyond the heavens. So new and different was this star from all the others, on earth it produced astonishment, and in the skies it seemed that the moon and sun and all the heavenly bodies gathered in chorus about this great, new light. Throughout all the world there was perplexity, for in the wisdom of the ancients such a star could mean only one thing.

And in the dark realms, there was tumult, anger, and fear. For now all the evil power of magic arts was to be dissolved. Every chain that spiritual wickedness wraps around its victims was to be broken. Man's ignorance of God was to be destroyed. And the old order of sin, which governs the kingdom of Death, was to crumble.

Yes, it was certain—God was becoming manifest in human form, bringing the dawn of a new eternal Kingdom of Life. All of creation began to tremble at once. The destruction of Death, which holds all matter in its chill grip, had begun. *Death was dying, and Life was being born!*

And a cry came from the Virgin and the child together, a cry that echoed into this world out from the realm of heaven . . . out from the deep mysteries of God's heart.

Ignatius of Antioch,
LETTER TO THE
EPHESIANS

18

Offering Sight to the Blind

*T*his is what God the L<small>ORD</small> says, ". . . I will make you
. . . a light for the Gentiles, to open eyes
that are blind. . . ."

Isaiah 42:5–7

*P*eter [said], ". . . God made a choice . . . that the
Gentiles might hear from my lips
the message of the gospel and believe. . . .
[And God] purified their hearts by faith."

Acts 15:7, 9

*Y*ou have attacked me with empty words,
Autolychus. You have threatened me by the power
of your gods, which means little to me because they
are only wood and stone, hammered and cast,
neither hearing nor seeing—dead idols, the work of
men's hands! And you "accuse" me of being a

Christian, as if being a Christian is a damning thing to be.

As to charges, I answer clearly: *I am a Christian.* And I gladly bear this name, which is the scorn of men, and loved by God. My only hope is that I will serve Him well all the days of my life under this name: Christian. For it is not hard, as you suppose, to bear this name for God, though we are being persecuted, imprisoned, tortured, and killed everywhere. This we count to His glory. No doubt you think this is hard for us to bear because you yourself are as yet of no use to God.

Most recently you have arrogantly challenged me, saying, "Show me your God."

I say, "Consider your soul—your inner man—which cannot be seen and yet is real." Show me your soul, I say, and I will show you God. Though you may not yet be aware of it, the eyes of your soul have the ability to see—that is, to perceive the qualities of Him who is invisible. And the ears of your soul have the ability to perceive His voice as He calls in your heart. By these—the eyes and ears within, which are opened by faith—we behold God.

To this point, Autolychus, the eyes of your soul are overspread with the tarnish of your sins and wicked deeds, so you are not able to perceive any light from heaven, which might reveal God to you in your inner man. That is because the soul within you is like a mirror, and if it is covered with rust it is impossible to catch a glimpse of anything in it. But if it is made clean, burnished to a shine, then you may behold the image of God in the only place where He can truly reveal himself to you, so you will believe with true conviction—that is, in your soul.

What is this tarnish I speak of? Tell the truth— do you not commit some of these acts, like the rest of your pagan friends: adultery, stealing, corrupting young boys, insolence against authorities, the slander of innocent people, angry brawling, envy, pride, coveting, selling your children to the temple priests, refusing to help your aged parents, wasting your own life in frivolous parties?

You boldly say, "Show me your God."

But God cannot show himself to someone who corrupts his own soul, not unless that man is willing first to have his soul made clean.

So I urge you, "Repent." Turn to God from your unbelief, call upon Him to forgive your sins by His mercy. Plead with Him to shed the light of His grace in your heart. For your own evil has spread corruption, like the discharge of a disease, over the eyes of your soul.

Only when you repent will you see and hear Him with your heart, as Christians are empowered by grace to do.

Theophilus of Antioch,
REPLY TO AUTOLYCHUS

19

The Act of Faith

*Faith by itself, if it is not accompanied
by action, is dead.*

James 2:17

Still you persist, Autolychus, in demanding
that I show you my God. You say you want to
know Him—then look all around you.

. . . Consider this world, and nature, which
inspires your worship of those false gods. Whose
wisdom created such order in all things? From the
vast systems of the stars that move across the sky to
mark the signs and seasons, to the great hidden
wells underground whose currents break out to
water the earth—oh, just open your heart and you
will know there is a God above all gods, above all
creation, who created such intricate design!

. . . By His good will, Autolychus, you are
enabled to use the voice that spits out your threats.
It is by His will that you have breath in your lungs!
. . . Autolychus, our God called you yourself into
being. For He created the very means by which you

were made in your mother's womb. He was present at the day of your birth, to guide you safely into this life. . . .

If only you would redirect your anger and your will. Stop trying to prove our God does not exist. Prove Him, and see that He does.

If just once your soul would catch a glimpse of Him, who is so above anything created, you will at once desire to live a pure life. You will understand why we so gladly set ourselves apart to serve Him alone. Like us, you would gladly change your behavior. You would leave your boastful, self-seeking life of pleasure behind and be pleased to live in loving service to both God and man.

. . . Though this is not what you want to hear, it is the only real answer to your question: *You may see God by faith*—the kind that comes as you fully commit yourself to Him.

For *faith* is the first principle in all things. Even the farmer must believe that his seed, which is so tiny, has the ability to grow a new crop to fill his barns. And *acting on your faith* is the second principle, proving that your belief is true. For the farmer must not only believe his seed can produce a new crop, he must act. And he does so by committing his seed to the ground, where the kernel dies in order to produce new life.

You who challenge me—I challenge you: Cast your soul to the earth before Christ, like a seed that is willing to die in order to be raised to this new life. Let your old corruptible life go. Let the Holy

Spirit clothe you inwardly with holiness and with life that is incorruptible.

What are you waiting for? Are you afraid what I am saying might be true? Or are you afraid to turn your back on this corrupted world with its false pleasures—afraid that if you look with your heart you might really see Him whom you have ridiculed? Are you fearful that your stubborn pride will be exposed?

Theophilus of Antioch,
REPLY TO AUTOLYCHUS

20
Ruled in Wisdom

In wisdom there is a spirit . . . [that is] kindly towards men . . . unerring, untouched by care, all-powerful, all-surveying, and permeating all intelligent, pure, and delicate spirits. . . . [Wisdom] is the brightness that streams from everlasting light, the flawless mirror of the active power of God and the image of his goodness. . . . [Wisdom] enters into holy souls, and makes them God's friends and prophets, for nothing is acceptable to God but the man who makes his home with wisdom.

Wisdom of Solomon 7:22–23, 26–28,
New English Bible

*This is what the Sovereign LORD . . . says:
". . . Although the Lord gives you the bread of adversity and the water of affliction, your teachers will be hidden no more; with your own eyes you will see them. Whether you turn to the right or to the left, your ears will hear a voice behind you, saying, 'This is the way; walk in it.' "*

Isaiah 30:15, 20–21

Be careful that you don't become puffed up by your own wisdom and understanding—this is the message that comes to us throughout Proverbs. In everything you do, in all that happens to you in life, acknowledge that there is a wisdom at work that's far higher than your own.

And so I tell you, seek God first, and ask Him to show you what He is about in every circumstance that comes into your life.

This is difficult for the human soul to grasp. Rebels that we are, we do not like the idea of submitting ourselves to be governed by anybody. And when hard circumstances come—things we perceive as painful or challenging—we never want to accept that God is still at work bringing His good plans to pass. We are like children, not wanting to accept medicine or food that will help us, just because it is not to our taste.

So the writer of Proverbs strengthens his point, again and again. He tells us not to be wise in our own eyes. By that he means to say, do not be guided by your own perceptions. Don't be unwilling to accept God's higher view of your circumstances, and learn patient endurance, by which your faith is provided. And do not be unwilling to give your life to fulfill His purposes and plans in the world, plans that began long before you were born, purposes that will be worked out after you are gone.

The temptation to *pride* lies in wait, constantly. Pride is not mere boastfulness. It hides quietly in the heart that believes it is better to live out from under the government of God, our good Sovereign. Do not resist Him and His workings. Still the voice of resistance within you. Trust Him. Seek Him. Let Him teach you His ways and guide you in the paths He has ordained for your life.

If we resist and seek our own way, we abandon His rule over us. Fools, we wind up opposing God—impiously boasting that we don't need God's help, or that we don't like His way with us. All because He hasn't seen fit to do things our way. Wisdom speaks, reminding us that the reverent respect for God's love and manifold understanding will keep us from such evil.

I urge you—walk this higher path of wisdom. Accept the discipline of a life that is governed by wisdom higher than your own views. Understand that God is love—and that He loves you. Accept the fact that He is always at work to straighten out every bit of crookedness in our sin-bent hearts. Like a good father, the Lord chastens those He loves.

Sometimes, for instance, He causes pain to enter our lives. You must seek Him during these times to see if He is using pain to teach and train you. If so, He will make it plain. If nothing else, the wise person knows that pain can cause you to press deeper into God—that is, into a more complete dependence upon Him—where you find sublime comfort of soul that lifts you above all anguish.

All of God's ways of government, whether of pain or joy, are useful in directing our souls to the peaceful pastures in spirit. For there our souls find rest, even when we cannot see where our Shepherd is leading us—even when the path ahead appears dark to our natural eyes. The more you come to rest in Him, the more fully you will enter into Life— that is, the kind of spiritual life that even death cannot touch.

. . . You now have in brief the foundation of our Christian spiritual philosophy. Learn to walk this upward path of wisdom. Pursue God in all things with an open heart, ready to be taught, ready to follow. As you practice wisdom, you will notice a change in your soul. You will go beyond merely seeking right understanding, and will pass into the place in spirit where you are simply a friend to God—a friend, I say, whose life is under the wise care and direction of the King and Ruler of all.

This is why I tell you, practice the kind of spiritual discipline that brings your soul, each day, under the government of God.

Clement of Alexandria,
MISCELLANEOUS TEACHINGS

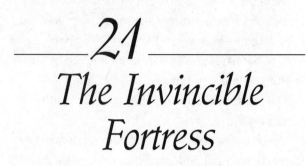

21
The Invincible Fortress

He who fears the LORD has a secure fortress.

———

Proverbs 14:26

O LORD . . . You hem me in—behind and before; you have laid your hand upon me. Such knowledge is . . . wonderful. . . .

———

Psalm 139:1, 5–6

How great is the kingdom of the mind! Its walls can be made strong to withstand the evil attacks of the world and our great Adversary.

In order to become strong within—strong in clinging to God, strong in turning away evil—you must make it a practice to purge earthly fears from your mind . . . and the thought that there is any security that comes from this world.

This is what the world looks like:

. . . Imagine that you are standing on the highest peak of a lofty mountain range. From there you can look down on things far below you. Beneath your gaze lie clouds as they drift and eddy, and rivers as they bend. . . .

Below, you also see . . . the roads clotted with robbers . . . wars scattered across the lands . . . the ground everywhere wet with blood . . . bribery and injustice ruling the judges in their courts. . . . In the cities, the gladiators are well-fed and exercised that they may use their brawn to inflict more pain on innocent wretches so that wicked, heartless crowds can enjoy themselves . . . fathers, mothers, brothers, and sisters must look on as those they love are butchered. . . . In the theaters, sexual debauchery has become entertainment . . . men are emasculated, and women are become men. . . .

But up where you stand, you are entirely alone, beyond the reach of all harm and danger.

This is a wonderful dream, you say, but we are still in this world. Yes, that's true.

So I tell you, your soul can only find peace and security one way. For some Christians teach that we should withdraw from the world. But I say that isn't enough—for evil will come and find you. And it isn't enough to tell yourself, "I simply won't think about the cares and dangers of this life." What good does it do to pretend you are blind?

Instead, make it your constant practice to lift the eyes of your soul from earth to heaven. Anchor your hope in heaven—for there is no unshakable ground here on earth, no security here. This world and all that is in it is passing away.

There are many Christians who receive the gift of the Spirit and of salvation, but they fail to receive the rest of their inheritance in Christ—which includes a mind and heart that is spiritually fortressed against the world. Because they remain of two minds—half hoping in the world, half hoping in God—they are constantly tossed about, assailed by the whims and tempers of fickle people, thrown by changing events. Too often they make the mistake of turning away from God when hardship comes and run back to the world, even returning to a lightless life of doubt and unbelief.

But when your mind is fixed on God, our eternal, unshakable hope, you are standing very near to Him—next to His very heart. Then is God your fortress. And nothing the world can do to you, nothing the world can tempt you with, can breach the walls of your inner man. Even the subtlest temptation, clothed in the grandest disguise, cannot enter your soul to disturb its peace.

He who is greater than the world can crave nothing and fear nothing that the world brings. This is the separation in heart unto God that the apostles recommend. . . .

As the sun shines, as the day gives light, as the spring flows, as the shower spreads sweet moisture—in this way the heavenly Spirit of peace infuses itself into our inner man. When the soul fixes its gaze into heaven, there it finds the One who created it. Then it rises higher than the sun, far transcending all earthly power. And we begin to be what we believe ourselves to be.

You are called into heavenly warfare—to win the world, and to win the freedom of your own soul from the snares of this lower world. If you want to win this spiritual battle, learn to practice this discipline I have taught you.

Cyprian,
FIRST EPISTLE

22
If Christ Is Not Raised . . .

If Christ has not been raised, our preaching is useless
and so is your faith. . . . The body that is sown is
perishable, it is raised imperishable; it is sown in
dishonor, it is raised in glory; it is sown in weakness, it
is raised in power; it is sown a natural body, it is raised
a spiritual body.

1 Corinthians 15:14, 42–44

[Some] were tortured [for their faith] and refused to be
released, so that they might gain a better resurrection.

Hebrews 11:35

I am so glad to hear of your bravery and patient
endurance—which shows how firmly your souls
are seated in heavenly places, even as your bodies
suffer torture. . . .

As you now know, the spiritual combat has

increased. And I'm overjoyed to see that in you, the combatants, the glory of God has increased also.

. . . As soldiers of Christ, in divine encampment, I encourage you: Do not let any of the world's allurements deceive you, and undermine the incorruptible ground of heaven on which your faith stands. Let no threats stir fear in you. Let no tortures defeat you.

Remember that "the one who is in you is greater than the one who is in the world" (1 John 4:4). And physical punishment cannot do more to crush you than God's protection can do to lift your spirit beyond reach of suffering. Follow bravely after the brothers and sisters who have gone before. What examples of faith and spiritual virtue they are! They fought the good fight in spirit, until the battle gave way to them.

. . . For their faith was powerfully, grandly displayed as they stood against the emissaries of evil who inflicted greater and greater torture. How long they labored in the fight as affliction grew more severe. And in the end their faith was not thrown down—far from it. They rejoiced at their deaths, knowing that death ushered them into the presence of the Lord more quickly.

Listen to the testimony of those present. They speak with utmost admiration for the heavenly contest—for indeed, this was a contest between the Spirit of Christ, and the spirit of this world. Though evil pressed our brothers to speak against Christ, they spoke *for* Him, and freedom sounded in their voices. Though they were bare of weapons to defend themselves, they were armed with weapons of faith. The tortured were more brave than the torturers, who shook with fear as they performed their horrible task. . . .

And the blood that flowed freely floods and quenches the fires of anger and persecution. In truth, it drowns the flames of hell itself. . . .

I want you to remember the words of our brother Mappalicus. The proconsul himself sat there watching, enjoying our brother's torments, waiting for him to renounce Christ. Instead, a voice filled with the Holy Spirit poured from the martyr's mouth, saying, "Do you want to see a contest?— then you will see one!"

So the heavenly contest was engaged. And this servant of God was crowned. . . .

As the Apostle Paul has told us, some run races so they can win a trophy that will decay—a crown that will wither. But the crown we will receive is eternal. (See 1 Corinthians 9:24–25.)

. . . If you are called out to the battle, if the day of your personal contest comes, join in the fight boldly. Stand firm in your faith, knowing that you are under the loving eye of a present Lord. By standing strong in His name, you will attain a share in His glory.

The glory I am speaking of is not mere honor, but something greater. For as you stand strong in faith in your suffering, you will find that He is not the kind of Lord who stands by and watches His servants struggling.

No, He does not leave you alone against the enemy. He himself will arise in you, present by the Holy Spirit, to engage with us in the battle. . . .

Cyprian,
EIGHTH EPISTLE

23

Living Stones, Fitted Together

As you come to [Christ], the living Stone—rejected by men but chosen by God and precious to him—you also, like living stones, are being built into a spiritual house to be a holy priesthood, offering spiritual sacrifices acceptable to God through Jesus Christ.

1 Peter 2:4–5

Do not grieve the Holy Spirit of God, with whom you were sealed [into the Church] for the day of redemption. Get rid of all bitterness, rage and anger, brawling and slander, along with every form of malice. Be kind and compassionate to one another, forgiving each other, just as in Christ God forgave you.

Ephesians 4:30–32

[Ignatius' comments]

You are the living stones in the Father's spiritual temple (1 Peter 2:5). And you are being

shaped and fitted into the sacred dwelling of God—
that is, His Church.

I will tell you how this shaping takes place.

You must be lifted up from this earth, this life,
as by a crane. By that I mean you must follow the
way of the *cross*, in which you exchange your lesser
will for God's higher will. Your inner man can only
escape its natural self-centeredness and live
according to God's spiritual design—no matter
what it costs you—as you are pulled up out of
yourself by the "rope" of the Holy Spirit. In this
way, the Spirit lifts you to the cross—for you cannot
lift yourself—and there you exchange your old way
of seeing and doing and living for a new way, in
God.

For your part, let faith be your upward guide—I
am speaking of spiritual vision, by which you fix
the eyes of your soul on Christ. Love is all you need
to strengthen you as you journey this higher
pathway: Love for God, and His love in you for
others.

Now remember I am talking to you about taking
your place in the building that is of God. And the
other stones in this building will not fit easily
against you at first. Your attitude should be this: We
are all friends and companions on the way. And no
one must think of himself as greater or less than
anyone else.

Each one of you is the bearer of God, and a
bearer of the holy virtues shown us in Christ. Each
one of you is like a small chapel, part of the great

cathedral which is God's mystical Church. Let your only adornment be in spirit, then, as you obey only the voice of Jesus our Lord.

I know you have already entered the spiritual Church, because you love nothing in this worldly life, only God.

Pray, and do not give up, where it comes to others in the Church—remember, just like you they are in the process of being shaped and fitted by God into His dwelling: Pray that your brothers in Christ may also understand how they may imitate God in Christ. Let them be instructed by the gentleness, meekness, kindness, and humility they see in you—not merely by your words, or the correctness of your doctrines.

So when a brother is angry with you—you be mild. When they are strong-willed, self-centered, and boastful—you be humble. When they abuse you—commit yourself to praying for them. When they are double-minded, or deceitful—for even fellow Christians can act like perfect children of the devil at times—you stand firm in a spiritual faith.

Even if a brother should be cruel to you, be gentle. Don't imitate them, imitate Christ. Teach your brothers by forbearing their foolishness and lack of spiritual maturity: be eager to lead them by living in the Spirit of Christ (1 Thessalonians 1:6).

Remain in Christ, then. Let the Holy Spirit lift you to the cross—and beyond, to the place where your inner man stands, raised with Christ. Let the Spirit purify you, by overruling and directing the reactions of your old lower nature. In this way you will grow to be like Christ—and you will destroy the works of the devil as he tries to tear apart the spiritual home of God.

I tell you, this manner of living with each other is urgent. For in this way, God comes through us His people to inhabit the earth.

Ignatius,
LETTER TO THE
EPHESIANS

24
Asking for Money

You do not have, because you do not ask. When you ask, you do not receive, because you ask with wrong motives, that you may spend what you get on your pleasures.

James 4:2–3

I am very disturbed at the news you send me—especially what you have told me about Valens, who was appointed elder among you in Philippi. I am disturbed, I say, because he has seriously misunderstood the office that was entrusted to him.

I exhort you, then, dear brothers and sisters in Christ, to resist the love of money. Be pure in your spirits, and be trustworthy. Run from all evil.

It is well for you to ask me—"How can a man who cannot govern his own soul tell us that we are supposed to be self-controlled?"

Anyone who does not keep himself from the love of money is spiritually blind indeed. His soul is veiled, and he cannot see God, who is the true source of all good things, the giver of good gifts and provisions for His children. A person like this may claim with his lips that he worships the true God, and even claim he is a spiritual leader—but the truth of his soul's state lies open to God: He is an idolater.

I warn you. I plead with you to understand! If you fall back into this state you will be treated by God as if you were a heathen gentile, still in spiritual darkness. For though you give lip service to our teachings about the spiritual kingdom and new life that is your inheritance, in your actions you show that you do not comprehend that God blesses us sometimes because He has judged us fit to wisely handle His blessings—not using them to heap comforts on ourselves, but carefully in service of His kingdom.

You have been told by Paul, and reminded by dear Clement and myself, that in the world to come you will be asked to judge, even between angels (1 Corinthians 6:2–3). How will you attain to this office, if in your judgment you fall, like some among you?

I say this, thinking of the wonderful report that Paul himself gave about you—even mentioning your fine character in Christ in his letter (Philippians 1:1–3). For when he labored among you, he boasted to us of you, holding you up as people who knew God and lived in the humble nature of Christ. And we looked to you for spiritual encouragement, for we did not yet know God.

So I am very, very unhappy about this elder and

his wife—may the Lord have mercy, and send the Holy Spirit to stir their souls to repentance!

I encourage you to help restore these, who were spiritual leaders, in a spirit of meekness. Do not strive or argue, like enemies. Lead them back into the spiritual faith by your own example. Consider them as weak members of your body, who have fallen by their error. Restore them gently, as you would rehabilitate one of your own limbs that has been crippled. . . .

I am confident that you know how to restore these people. For you are well-trained in the sacred writings of the apostles. And nothing of the nature of Christ—nothing of the truth—is hidden from you.

Polycarp of Smyrna,
LETTER TO THE
PHILIPPIANS

25
Our Purity

Train the younger women . . . to be self-controlled and pure. . . . Similarly, encourage the young men to be self-controlled. In everything set . . . an example . . . so that those who oppose you may be ashamed because they have nothing bad to say about us.

Titus 2:4–8

There are many among your citizens who have set accusations about us before you.

They claim that what we refer to as "love feasts" are spectacles of debauchery. . . .

But I know that you, O Emperor, have studied so as to excel in intelligence. Therefore, I appeal to your reason. Permit me to answer these charges.

You know that we Christians, who look only to God as the Ruler of our lives, long to be blameless and above reproach in His eyes. We struggle to bring every thought captive to Christ (2 Corinthians 10:5), not willing to entertain even the thought of sin.

Why? Because we do not believe that this

present life is our only life—we have been given new life from above, as a sign of our eternal life that is to come. If we did not stake our hope in this, then you might suspect us of sinning—for the man who fails to fix his heart on things above will indeed be a slave to flesh and blood, a slave to earthly gain and his own body's demands.

Further, we do not think for a minute that any act is performed in secret, though it is concealed from the eyes of all men. We know that God sees every action, every word, whether in broad daylight or under cover of darkness. More than that, because He is Light, He sees every thought and intent of the heart.

We are fully persuaded that, when this earthly life is over, we will be raised to another one—a life far better than this earthly life, in the heavenly realms that are now hidden from our eyes. Better, I say, because we will then dwell near God, with God. And in that life we will be free from all loss, change, pain, and grief. Though we will have new bodies (1 Corinthians 15:44), that life will be nothing like the one we now live in this fallen flesh. Or, if we fall with the rest of mankind, who refuse God's offer of new life in the Spirit, we will suffer the fire.

Finally, we know that God has made us higher than His other creations—so we are not like the beasts that we should simply die and be annihilated.

Given all this, is it likely that we would

willingly commit evil? Is it likely that we would hand ourselves over to the One who will judge all men, to be punished?

... As to the specific charges of immorality—I invite you to examine our lives. You will find that there are a great many men and women among us who, since their youth, have lived chaste and unmarried, spending their whole lives in service and prayer and in close communion with God. . . .

O Emperor, before you decide what you will do to us, think on all these things.

Athenagoras,
PLEA TO THE EMPEROR
MARCUS AURELIUS

26
God, Our Only Help

Of what value is an idol . . . he who makes it trusts in his own creation. . . . Can it give guidance [when] there is no breath in it? But the LORD is in his holy temple: let all the earth be silent before him.

Habakkuk 2:18–20

The LORD is good, a refuge in times of trouble. He cares for those who trust in him.

Nahum 1:7

Without doubt, this world is beautiful. It is excellent in its vast mountains, oceans, and plains—and in the sky above, where the stars and planets circle in perfect order.

Yet we must never worship anything in the creation. Nor any image derived from a created thing. We must worship only the One whose artifice brought all the heavens and the earth into existence, using only His Word.

Is it not so, O Emperor, with you and your subjects? . . . When they come to the palace they admire its beauty, but it is to you yourself that they bow in honor. You sovereigns create spectacular residences for yourselves—though it is not quite the same with God, our Sovereign. He did not need to create the universe in order to have some place to dwell.

Let me tell you what God is like.

God is, in himself, perfect and complete. He needs nothing. He is unapproachable light. He is Spirit, power, clearest reason.

If I were to describe this world's beauty as a fine instrument, sweetly tuned, and playing in perfect time—then it is the One who plays the instrument I love. You Romans, in your musical contests, never award the prize to the lute, but to the lutist—why do you worship the thing made, and not the Maker?

I will warn you, as I warn my own brothers and sisters in Christ: Do not look to nature as your source of life and well-being, protection or happiness. All that is below heaven is made of matter, which is perishable. Do not mistake the tremendous powers of nature for the power of God—His might surpasses all the terrifying power of the seas, earthquakes, or winds of might.

I myself do not ask of matter what it does not have to give. Though sickness, or need, or hard circumstances appear to be whelming against me, I fix the eyes of my soul beyond them all. I look above to God himself. And I do not look to man, as if human favor, or skill, is any sure source of help. Nature and man—neither can do more than what God bids and empowers them to do, for good or ill. For life and all provision and our well-being lie with Him alone.

. . . Even Plato bears testimony to what I am saying—if you refuse to listen to me, listen to him! He said, "that which we call heaven and earth have received many blessings from the Father, yet everything in them is made of matter. So they are not free from change."

Therefore, even though I admire the creation for its beauty, I do not worship the creation. Nor do I worship anything made in the semblance of nature, or look to created things for my help—most definitely *not* to an idol. For the law of change, dissolution, and decay lies over all.

Please listen to what I am telling you, for your own sake. . . .

Athenagoras,
PLEA TO THE EMPEROR
MARCUS AURELIUS

112

27
Two Paths

Woe to those who call evil good and good evil. . . .

Isaiah 5:20

*The LORD gives wisdom. . . . Wisdom will save you
from the ways of wicked men, from men whose words
are perverse. . . . Do not set foot on the path of the
wicked or walk in the way of evil men. . . . Put away
perversity from your mouth. . . . Let your eyes look
straight ahead. . . . Make level paths for your feet.*

Proverbs 2:6, 12; 4:14, 24, 26

I must speak candidly to you, brothers and
sisters in Christ, about the perverse behavior of the
pagans. For though we live right among them in
this world, we must resist all the pull to imitate
them.

Earlier, I cautioned you not to imitate the pagan
men, who make themselves smooth and who paint
themselves in order to attract other men. Nor to
imitate their women, who lust for other women. . . .

113

Now I offer another serious warning: They have so perverted and degraded sexuality that it is no longer the sacred intercourse between man and woman which God intended.

Sexuality is treated like a common act—no different than buying fruit in the street. Lewdness fills their plays and entertainment. Men and women brag about their sexual conquests, as if each encounter is a trophy to be exhibited. Lechery has become like a public institution—for though the society is founded on so-called "right philosophical principles," yet everyone knows where to find a prostitute. And the authorities look the other way.

Here is the sorriest part of this wickedness: These people, so eager to enjoy their sexual "freedom," create children from their many encounters. And when an infant is not wanted, it is abandoned, according to the pagan customs, in the street outside the home of the mother. The pagan priests, who move like carrion up and down the city, accept the child as a "servant to the gods." And the child is raised in debauched fashion.

So it comes about that the men of our day wind up lying with their own sons and daughters— unaware that they have even brought a child into the world. . . .

These things, the pagan lawmakers of our day allow. People sin legally, though of course the authorities will not call it sin. "People have the right to indulge in pleasures. Who are we to prohibit them?"

. . . I admire the Roman lawmakers of old. When the society was founded, they detested such low conduct. For they understood the need for men and women to develop self-control. For without righteousness, fallen humanity has no bounds. . . .

If you allow yourself to begin thinking like the men of our day, you have already begun to follow evil people down the wrong path. . . . If you are not careful, you will leave the path of life. . . .

Clement of Alexandria,
THE INSTRUCTIONS

28
Walking Among Angels

The angels are . . . spirit-messengers sent out to help and care for those who are to receive his salvation.

Hebrews 1:14, TLB

I want to talk with you about angels. . . .

When God created the angels, He gave them certain roles and offices. These include exercising providence for God over the things He created and ordered. So God himself rules over all things, and He is the only One who knows and understands the master pattern of all things; while certain aspects of creation are ruled by angels, who are yet subordinate to God and His plan.

Just as men have been given the will to choose between virtue and vice . . . so it is with the angels. Some have been diligent to serve Him, while others have been utterly faithless. Some continue in the offices for which He created them, doing the work He planned for them. While for others, the place and work God fashioned them for was not good enough—and so they chose to rebel.

These latter angels corrupted the pure spiritual nature with which they were created. It was not enough that they have a place in God's government, ruling from the invisible realm over physical matter—no, they lusted for that which was lower than their nature. I am not saying this on my own authority, but the authority of the prophets, who were instructed in these invisible events by the Spirit of God. (See Isaiah 14:12–15.)

So some of these angels became perverted. Despising the nature with which they were created, they lusted for human flesh. . . . These angels have fallen from the realm of heaven, then, and now they haunt the air and earth. No longer able to rise to heavenly things . . . they have taken on the nature of whatever appetite they indulged. . . .

And now, these demons are the forces that influence men, drawing them to the worship of idols and the so-called "old powers" of the earth. They incite men to offer blood sacrifices, licking their lips at the human gore.

But we Christians do not fear the demons, or what they may do to us—for we are in Christ, protected in spirit by His presence. We do not fear the knife of the pagan priest, nor fear any bodily harm that threatens us.

Instead, we remain on guard for the sake of our souls. For when a demon plots against any man, he begins by inflicting some hurt upon the mind—

causing him to distrust the true God, and to be angry toward Him.

We guard our souls so that they do not become ground on which the enemy can take a stand. Our soul's defense lies in renewing our minds, until we are at rest in knowing this:

God, who is perfect in goodness, governs every matter that concerns us. And from the highest heaven, where He dwells above all powers and principalities, He sends His ministering angels to help us as we work out our salvation.

Athenagoras,
PLEA TO THE EMPEROR
MARCUS AURELIUS

29

Free

Jesus [said], ". . . a slave has no permanent place in the family, but a son belongs to it forever. So if the Son sets you free, you will be free indeed."

John 8:34–36

God sent His prophets to make it clear from the beginning what He wanted from His people. That is, a home and dwelling place for His Spirit, in us.

At first, He told the people of Israel to offer sacrifices. But that was only to be a shadow of what was to come—a symbol, a story acted out over and over, a reminder that a perfect sacrifice must one day be offered. Sacrifice was necessary to free the people from their enslavement to sin. They were never to mistake the outward act of sacrifice, however, for God was always trying to speak to them about the inward preparation of the heart— and about spiritual sacrifice.

God tried to teach them, saying:

"The multitude of your sacrifices—what are they

to me? Stop bringing meaningless offerings!"
(Isaiah 1:11, 13).

He did this to prepare His people for the time
when He would set aside the first law, which was,
as I said, a vague shadow of what was to come.
And then Jesus came to teach us how to perfectly
fulfill the law in spirit. This law does not bind or
force us, as the heavy yoke of the old law did. This
law sets us free to live our lives in Christ—resting
in the love of the Father, as He did.

No, the new law of life and liberty is not
burdensome, it is light. For this is what the
prophets began to command as they tried to show
the people the attitude of heart God was trying to
create in them:

" . . . show mercy and compassion to one
another" (Zechariah 7:9)—which is to say *forgive one
another*. And now we *can* forgive because God has
told us to leave justice, retribution, and recompense
in His hands. If we are His children, we will simply
trust Him to do so—if not in this life, then in the
life to come. . . .

Again, He says:

"The sacrifices of God are a broken spirit; a
broken and contrite heart" (Psalm 51:17)—meaning
that we are to be broken of our self-centered ways,
become teachable and, like children, ready to
follow His ways instead of our own. . . .

And again He addresses the spirit of the matter,
saying,

"Is this the kind of fast I have chosen, only a

day for a man to humiliate his flesh?" (Isaiah 58:5, author's phrasing). Rather, "Is this not the kind of fast I have chosen? . . . Loose every bond of injustice. . . . Distribute your food to the hungry. . . . Release the downtrodden with forgiveness . . . clothe the naked . . . bring the homeless into your home. . . ." (vv. 6–7).

For God wanted much more than outward obedience to laws and a system of sacrifices. He wanted us to know Him, to rest within Him, as children in the all-surrounding care of a good father. He always planned to place the dawn light of His presence in us:

"Then your light will break forth like the dawn, and your healing will quickly appear; then your righteousness will go before you, and the glory of the Lord will be your rear guard. Then when you cry to the Lord for help, He will answer quickly, 'Here am I' " (Isaiah 58:8–9, author's phrasing).

. . . God has always meant to bring His straying children back into His fatherly care. So our Father, the Patient One, prepared a way for us to come into new life, in the Beloved (see Ephesians 1:6)—and that way is to love Him with all our hearts, in childlike trust and innocence.

For this reason, protect the simple faith that is in your hearts. Do not let anyone lead you back into legalism, as some false teachers are trying to do. For if you let yourself slip under the law, it will crush and destroy the work of the Spirit as He frees you by pouring out God's grace within.

But you must continue to rest in His grace—sacrificing your pride. That means you must give up your tendency to excuse yourself from obeying the command of God to love freely as He loves. And it means you must give up your tendency to justify yourself or shift the blame to someone else when you have sinned, or ignored God.

If instead you rest in His grace, allowing Him to turn you out of your prison of self-centeredness into the beautiful freedom of childlike obedience, then you will be free indeed.

Barnabas,
LETTER TO ALL THE
CHURCHES

30

"You Know the
Way. . . ."

*Jesus [said], "The hour has come for the Son of Man to
be glorified. I tell you the truth, unless a kernel of wheat
falls to the ground and dies, it remains only a single
seed. But if it dies, it produces many seeds. The man
who loves his life will lose it, while the man who hates
his life in this world will keep it for eternal life.
Whoever serves me must follow me; and where I am,
my servant also will be. . . ." [Jesus said to Peter,] "You
know the way to the place where I am going."*

John 12:23–26; 14:4

My friends in Christ, I fear your love for me.
For it may yet harm my spirit.

It is easy for you to do whatever you wish. But
it will be difficult for me to do what I long to do—
which is to reach God—if you do not stop asking
me to remain with you. . . .

All I ask of you is this: Pray that the grace of
God will empower me from within so that I may be

strong to do what I know I must. For I know by the Spirit that I am called to not only *say* I am a Christian, but to *prove* it. For if I am found faithful, then I deserve to be called one of Christ's own. My time is coming, friends, when I must be faithful to the call and disappear from this world.

You are wrong if you think I am heavy-spirited about this. I am delighted! Because nothing in this visible world seems good to me now—not compared to the vision of Christ our God which I see with the eyes of my soul. I see Him clearly, risen above, and in the Father.

Do not make the mistake of thinking that Christianity is a matter of believing the right doctrines. Or being persuasive enough in your reasoning abilities that you can philosophically defend the Faith. Christianity is not a matter of believing in ideas that are "more right" than someone else's ideas. Rather, it is having the Spirit of Christ rise from within you, like the sweet fragrance of a flower that has been crushed, when you are hated and persecuted by the world.

I am writing to all the other churches, not only to you. As your overseer in Christ, I say: I am laying down my life for Christ willingly. Don't hinder me! Don't do an "inopportune favor" for me by making appeals.

Let me be food for the wild beasts—those in the stands and those in the arena! Offering my life in this way is not death to me. I lose nothing and gain eternal life in God.

I am the wheat of God. If I am ground by the teeth of wild beasts I will be found in the pure bread of Christ—following Him in the sacrifice He offered for the feeding of His spiritual body. . . .

If you offered me the whole earth and its kingdoms, I would say, "Where is the profit in these things, where my soul is concerned?" The worldly among you will not understand this. It profits my soul greatly to die, in order to feed the faith of those who are in Christ. To be king of the world is nothing in comparison.

In fact, I have already left you. In my solitude of prayer, my soul goes seeking Him who died for us. I cry after Him who rose for us. So great is my soul's longing, it's like the pain of a woman in labor.

Let me go, brothers. Don't prevent me from living by keeping me here in death. Don't give the world one who only wants to obey His heavenly calling and go to be with God. Don't lead me astray by begging me to stay here with you.

Let me imitate the passion of my God. . . .

If you truly have the Spirit of Christ in you, you will understand the love that drives me.

Ignatius of Antioch,
LETTERS TO THE
ROMANS

31
Imitating Christ

Paul, Silas, and Timothy, to the Church of the Thessalonians. . . . You became imitators of us and of the Lord; in spite of severe suffering, you welcomed the message with the joy given by the Holy Spirit. And so you became a model to all believers. . . .

1 Thessalonians 1:1, 6–7

The devil devises many evils against us. But—praise to God!—the devil can never triumph. For when God has called us on His path, even if it leads through the devil's territory, nothing can prevail over our souls.

I want to tell you about one—the most humble Polycarp, overseer of the churches—and his triumph over the evil one. But first I must offer a caution.

Do not be like Quintius, who recently came here from Phrygia. Even though no one sought his life, he began to talk some of the Christian brothers into offering themselves to the Romans. In fact, he pressured them into it. But after giving himself up for arrest, he saw the wild beasts—then it was a different matter. The proconsul had only to prod him a little, and he renounced Christ and offered a sacrifice to the Roman gods.

This kind of self-martyrdom, and self-punishment, is not what our Lord taught us in His Gospel. They are of the flesh.

On the other hand, consider our Polycarp, who was led by the Spirit through death to life. . . .

Because of Polycarp's excellent reputation, the evil-minded crowds became stirred to a frenzy. . . . "Bring Polycarp to us!" they shouted.

Polycarp was not disturbed in the least when the news came to him. He peacefully withdrew to a farm outside the city to seek the Lord on the matter. . . . There, in prayer and fasting, he was given a vision, in which he saw himself falling asleep on his pillow, surrounded in fire. . . .

Three days later, his whereabouts was betrayed to the authorities by a member of his own house. . . . Though Polycarp learned of the betrayal and could have escaped, he remained, speaking serenely to those fretting over him—"Peace! Let the Lord's will be done."

When his persecutors arrived, he greeted them at the door. Ordering food and drink for them, he asked only for one more hour of prayer to prepare himself. They were amazed and almost sorry that they were to arrest such a graceful, godly old man. . . .

As Polycarp was led into the stadium, a hideous

roar went up from the bloodthirsty crowd. As he entered, the Christians who were allowed to accompany him heard a loud voice from heaven, saying to him, "Be strong, Polycarp. Play the man."

The proconsul tried to persuade Polycarp to deny Christ. "You have lived a long life—don't you want to finish your days in peace? . . . Curse Christ, and I will let you live."

"I have served Him eighty-six years," Polycarp replied loudly. "In no way has He ever treated me unfairly. How can I blaspheme my King, who gave His life to save me?"

The proconsul became impatient. "Unless you change your mind, I will throw you to my wild beasts." Then he said, "I will have your body burned to ashes, in fire."

Polycarp said boldly, "Your fire burns for an hour and goes out. But you are ignorant of the fire of eternal judgment that awaits the wicked. . . . But why are you hesitating? Go ahead, do what you've planned to do." As he spoke, his voice filled with godly courage, and his face was infused with a light, as from heaven. . . .

As they forced him to disrobe, we remembered how we had always rushed to assist him. Not that he was feeble, but he had lived such a godly life that healing virtue sometimes passed from him, just from his touch.

They did not nail him to the stake in the center of the pyre. Rather they bound his hands behind him. . . . As they did, he looked up to heaven and prayed, "Lord God, Almighty One . . . I praise you! I bless you! I glorify you!"

When the fire was lit, the pitch caused it to roar instantly into a terrible flame. And we who were present saw a miracle.

The fire billowed around Polycarp like a sail filling with wind. And he was in the center of it— shining like gold or silver being refined. And a fragrant smell like incense filled the air. When the pagans saw that his body would not be kindled by the flames, the executioner took his life with a dagger. . . .

And the whole crowd murmured in amazement, that there is such a difference between those who do not believe in Christ and the elect.

From the Christians of Smyrna,
to the whole Church.

32
His Servants

When [the Lamb] opened the fifth seal [of the scroll he had taken from Him who sits on the throne], I saw under the altar the souls who had been slain because of the word of God and the testimony they had maintained. They called out in a loud voice, "How long, Sovereign Lord, holy and true, until you judge the inhabitants of the earth and avenge our blood?" . . . they were told to wait a little longer, until the number of their fellow servants and brothers who were to be killed . . . was completed.

Revelation 6:9–11

---

*W*e always pray for you that trial may not come your way. If so, the Lord's will be done. But it may be that peace will accompany you all your days.

No matter what you experience in this life—peace or hardships—set your will like iron to follow Christ. Keep your conscience pure. We do this by running away from sin and also by following after Christ as He goes before us, preparing the good works He has for each of us to do.

We know that some of you are sad that you were not called by the Lord to give your lives, like the martyrs. You think that perhaps you were not worthy to be His spokesmen to the world, or to enter into His presence by the high road.

The Lord knows your good hearts. He searches your hearts (Revelation 2:3) and knows how motivated you are to serve Him, in whatever way He asks. . . .

In order to win the crown of life, it is only necessary to be faithful to testify of Him—His forgiveness, His lordship over all—in whatever circumstances He leads you. He is your only judge, and not man. . . .

And so, put on the white robe of salvation, with joy, dignity, and honor. By that, I mean your part is to dress your spirits in the pure virtue of obedience and be like Christ. You already "robe" yourself in brilliant white by your works of charity, and by the unashamed way you speak for Christ at every opportunity. You need not worry that you have not put on the scarlet robes of the martyrs.

Among the flowers of heaven, which God wreaths into crowns for His victorious ones, there are blossoms both white and red—lilies and roses. (Do we not remind you of this, when we use them to adorn our churches?)

Humbly receive whatever crown has been fashioned for you—the white crown of good works well done as unto the Lord, or the scarlet crown of suffering.

Accept whatever task the Lord gives you, and whatever honor, as a good soldier in this spiritual contest between the powers of the world and Christ.

Cyprian,
EIGHTH EPISTLE

33
Coming Judgment

The present heavens and earth are reserved for fire,
being kept for the day of judgment and destruction
of ungodly men. . . . The Lord is not slow in keeping
his promise, as some understand slowness.
He is patient with you, not wanting anyone to perish,
but everyone to come to repentance.
But the day of the Lord will come like a thief.
The heavens will disappear with a roar;
the elements will be destroyed by fire.
Since everything will be destroyed in this way,
what kind of people ought you be?

2 Peter 3:7, 9–11

Jesus, whom we proclaim both God and man, was born for two purposes: He came for the benefit of those who would come to believe in Him—and to defeat the demons, those angels who had fallen from their first estate.

Even you unbelieving Romans do not need me to tell you that the power and name of Jesus conquer the darkness. With your own eyes you have seen demoniacs throughout the empire—and even there in Rome—driven out by Christians. This is the same Jesus of Nazareth who gave himself to be crucified under Pontius Pilate, the governor you appointed.

Yes, you have observed Christians driving out demons, when no one else could help the poor souls benighted by these terrible spirits. None of your exorcists and none of your magicians with their incantations and strange drugs could help these people at all.

Only the name and power of Jesus of Nazareth could deliver them.

For this reason—the defeat of Satan—God delays the day when the whole universe we see will convulse, and will dissolve in fire. He delays in order to complete His conquest of the fallen world through us His children—that is, Christians. For in us He has deposited the seed of life from above—a life more powerful to heal and save than the dark powers are to destroy and enslave.

God refrains himself from speaking the word that will close this present age. If He did not, it would be impossible for you to do the terrible things you do to those who love the Truth. And you yourselves are under the influence of demons, because they hate the Truth. . . . But we do not lay full blame on the powers of darkness for your behavior, nor does God. It is only because you resist God that the demons gain dominion over you. So much so that they influenced your forefathers to kill a man like Socrates—your own philosopher!—when he came close to discovering the Truth.

Since God has created both angels and men with free will, each will pay the just penalty in everlasting fire for the sins they commit. For each one of us is capable of choosing sin, or virtue. . . .

As God in His mercy delays judgment for *you*, will you not choose virtue?

Justin Martyr,
SECOND APOLOGY

34
All Flesh Will See Him

*"I know that my Redeemer lives, and that in the end he
will stand upon the earth. And after my skin has been
destroyed, yet in my flesh will I see God;
I myself will see him . . . and not another.
How my heart yearns within me!"*

Job 19:25–27

You pagans mock us for believing that the
body will be resurrected along with the spirit. Yet
that is indeed what we Christians believe: There
will be a joyous reunion of both body and spirit. . . .

You argue with us, saying our talk about the
resurrection of the body does not make rational
sense to you. "How can a man's spirit be reunited
with his body," you say, "when the body has
dissipated in the earth, or dissolved in the sea, or
been destroyed in fire?"

Our God created everything out of nothing.
With Him, nothing is impossible. He is entirely able

to draw together, from the ends of the earth, even the scattered molecules of our bodies.

As it has been revealed to us from above, we stand our ground and declare: As a final display of His power of fallen humanity, God *will* resurrect the body and reunite it with the spirit. Every one of us will be formed anew. . . .

But be careful that you do not spend your whole life wrangling over these intellectual arguments. You may waste your whole life claiming you are seeking truth, and never come to the knowledge of the One who is Truth (1 Timothy 1:6–7).

Though most men are too occupied with the crude things of this lower life, there is a higher use of the intelligent, rational mind. First, still all your clamoring thoughts. Then, fill your mind, and delight yourself, with silent contemplation of the One who is higher than our minds can conceive.

For this is what your spirit was created for—to fix its focus on God, and on His decrees. If only you will do this, you will find that everything we are telling you is indeed true. For God will come and reveal himself to your souls, and you will know that you were created to have eternal life . . . if you will choose Him who gives it.

Athenagoras,
On the Resurrection

35

The Kingdom Will Come

The kingdom will be the LORD's.

Obadiah 21

The wolf will lie with the lamb . . . and the lion will eat straw like the ox. . . . The infant will play near the hole of the cobra. . . . They will neither harm nor destroy on all my holy mountain, for the earth will be full of the knowledge of the LORD, as the waters cover the sea. In that day, the Root of Jesse will stand . . . the nations will rally to him, and his place of rest will be glorious.

Isaiah 11:6–10

I am concerned to see that the teachings of the heretics and pagans have influenced many Christians, particularly in the matter of the resurrection and the life to come.

Jesus taught us about a Kingdom in which there

138

will be no more corruption. In this Kingdom, those who are found worthy in Christ will gradually become accustomed to receiving the fullness of God. Since wrong doctrines have infected the churches, it is necessary that I make sure you hear the truth.

The righteous must rise first, at God's appearing, and they will inherit all the promises He made to our fathers. This will take place in this present order, and after this will come the judgment. This must be so because of the just nature of God.

Therefore, those who labored for the Faith will be rewarded for their work in this world. And those who patiently endured suffering will, likewise, be rewarded for their steadfastness in this world. And those who were put to death for the love of God will be made wonderfully alive again in this world. And those who gave up their lives in prisons for the Faith will reign in this world.

For all things belong to God. It is right for this whole created realm to be restored to its pristine state, as He first planned. It is right for this creation to serve His just ones out of the rich goodness He fashioned into it, at the time He commanded it into being.

The Apostle Paul made this clear in his letter to the Romans, when he wrote:

"The creation waits in eager expectation for the sons of God to be revealed. For the creation was subjected to frustration, not by its own choice, but by the will of the one who subjected it, in hope that the creation itself will be liberated from its bondage to decay and brought into the glorious freedom of the children of God" (8:19–21).

All this *must* come to pass, for when God makes a promise it is firm. And He promised Abraham saying,

"Lift up your eyes from where you are and look north and south, east and west. All the land that you see I will give to you and your offspring forever. . . . Go, walk through the length and breadth of the land, for I am giving it to you" (Genesis 13:14–15, 17). Yet Abraham did not inherit so much as a footprint of the land for his own; he and his family were always strangers there. . . .

Yes, God promised Abraham full inheritance of the land, but he did not see the promise fulfilled. That is because God waits to fulfill His word until all of Abraham's children are born. Abraham waits to receive the promise along with all of His seed. This includes us, the Church, for the spiritual seeds of faith were sown in us through his faith. And now we too are born into the family of God.

Think of it—in that day, when the family of God on earth is completed, we will inherit the promise— the whole world—together. . . . As Jesus said, "Blessed are the meek, for they will inherit the earth" (Matthew 5:5).

Jesus also told us, "Whoever has left fields, or houses, or parents, or brothers, or sons for my sake, will receive a hundredfold *in this world*, and in the world to come will inherit eternal life." (See

140

Matthew 19:29, Irenaeus' comment.)

And where are the hundredfold rewards in this age? Where are all the dinners we offer to the poor, which Jesus promised to repay in lavish banquets? (See Luke 14:12–14.) These things will happen on the earth in the times of the Kingdom . . . when the Sabbath comes for the just, in which there is no earthly work to do. Then a table will be prepared for us in the presence of God, and we will be fed with the food of heaven. . . .

Some of the elders among us remember how the Apostle John told them the many things Jesus said about the days of the Kingdom. How the vines will yield bountiful fruits, and the grain fields too. How the animals will no longer devour and fear each other, but will be in peace, and tame to man. . . .

Best of all, in this new order our bodies will always remain new. We will be able to talk with God himself! . . . As God said through Isaiah, "As the new heavens and the new earth that I will make endure before me . . . so will your name and descendants endure" (Isaiah 66:22).

Then those who are found worthy of heaven, in Christ, will be allowed into that eternal dwelling. . . . And the Savior will be seen again, and He will walk among us. . . .

Irenaeus,
AGAINST THE HERESIES

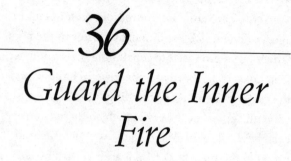

36
Guard the Inner Fire

Brothers, we do not want you to be ignorant. . . . For the Lord himself will come down from heaven, with a loud command. . . .

—————

1 Thessalonians 4:13, 16

You will be counted worthy of the Kingdom of God, for which you are suffering. God is just: He will pay back trouble to those who trouble you and give relief to you who are troubled. . . . This will happen when the Lord Jesus is revealed from heaven in blazing fire with his powerful angels.

—————

2 Thessalonians 1:5–7

Watch over the eternal life that has been planted in your soul, as a gardener tends seeds in the earth. For your faith is like a seed, charged with flame of eternal life. Don't let the fire of your faith go out. . . .

First, remain awake—that is, conscious of Christ—at all times. For no one knows the exact hour when He will return for us (Matthew 24:42).

Next, gather with other believers frequently. As you spend time together, seek the good things that feed your soul. . . .

In the last days, false prophets will come. Also men who will corrupt the Faith. . . . Men in the world will lose their senses, saying that it is good to go against natural laws that have stood through all time. Refusing to place themselves under God's laws, they will think nothing of persecuting men who only seek to live holy lives.

Then the one who deceives the whole world will appear. Those who know no better will claim, "He is the son of God!" Because he will give spiritual signs, and he will perform wonders. (See Mark 13:22; 2 Thessalonians 2:4, 9.) The earth will be given into his hands by God, and he will commit abominations—against God and man—like nothing that has ever been done before.

This will be allowed by God. Why? Because men will pull away from Him and His laws, and create a world without Him. And so He must pass it through His fire, as it were, to test the thing men have created. In this way, He will show men the truth about the "wisdom" that is without God. And many will not turn to the truth, even in the testing. Rather than turn to God, they will choose to let their souls perish.

But those who remain strong in the faith—

though the whole world turns against them—they will indeed be saved. They will be brought through the fiery testing, like gold that shines, by the One whom the world has cursed. . . .

And then the Lord will come. . . .

THE DIDACHE
(Teaching of the Apostles)

37
Pray for the Church

Pray in the Spirit on all occasions with all kinds of prayers and requests . . . be alert and always keep on praying for all the saints.

Ephesians 6:18

Many among you are weak and sick, and a number of you have fallen asleep. But if we judged ourselves, we would not come under judgment. When we are judged by the Lord, we are being disciplined so that we will not be condemned with the world.

1 Corinthians 11:30–32

I am sure, brothers, that you know how important it is to pray. I am pleased to hear that you pray all the time, laying all your needs before God.

But there is something we must pray about with

more urgency than our own personal needs. For we have come to the point where we must go beyond prayer, and begin to fast and cry out to God for His help.

I am referring to the spiritual disorder that is laying waste the flock of God. For many leaders have become lax, and many believers also. Many think nothing of sinning. They have forgotten the Way of the Lord, ignoring the path that leads to heaven. And so, spiritual decay is crippling the body of Christ.

For Jesus came to show us the way to the Father, through childlike trust and obedience. Oh, but this is not what we want! Those born into "better" families will not associate with "poor" Christians. Far from seeking heavenly treasure, we run after money. If there is a disagreement over the slightest thing, it escalates into all-out warfare and churches are torn apart by factions. Where Jesus taught us to be simple, and to be satisfied with the simple goodness of life, that's not good enough for us! We renounce the world with our lips, and then struggle to grab everything this world offers—mesmerized and falling into the devil's snares on every hand. When some so-called earthly blessing is shaken, we mock God for not being "strong enough" to protect our property for us.

Brothers, the body of Christ has fallen into a dangerous state of spiritual illness. . . . And now that shaking and trials have come, we must see them for what they are.

When we love the world, we despise the Lord's commandment—"Follow me." For in following Him, we overcome the world. If instead we run after the world, the enemy has power to do great harm among us. He easily overwhelms those who have become weak-eyed in spiritual vision—and lame in their spiritual walk, so that they easily stumble in their faith when the first little bit of trouble falls in their path. Then the enemy casts his net over these weak wanderers, dragging them away from the path altogether.

This is happening everywhere because Christians are not being armed with a spiritual faith, which would make them strong and armed for our subtle warfare against the world and the flesh.

So I am writing to you, commanding you to stop praying only for your own personal needs. But pray—fast, and cry out to God—for the spiritual restoration of the whole Church. . . . Lift up your eyes from the earth. Fix them on heaven, or the entrapments of the earth will draw you away as well. . . .

If the Lord looks upon us, sifts our hearts, and finds that we have returned to Him as humble children; if He sees us at peace with each other, not vying for attention or leadership over each other; if He sees us respecting His authority and power again; if we are corrected by our mistakes and stop defending our worldliness; if by our new spirit we overcome the divisions that tear us—then the Lord will protect us from the enemy, who is the Destroyer.

Remember, though the Lord disciplines, His pardon and love quickly follow . . . when we are willing to be corrected.

Cyprian,
SEVENTH EPISTLE

38
The Last Enemy

The last enemy to be destroyed is death.

1 Corinthians 15:26

The Lord taught us about the various rewards that will be given to those who serve Him, depending on their diligence.

He said that those who serve will reap a harvest—some will reap thirty, some sixty, and some a hundredfold (see Matthew 13:18–23). For their hearts were tender to receive His Word, the seed of our new life. And not only did they receive it, but they kept their hearts free of the weeds of sin and false teachings.

And so, as our lives produce different crops of righteousness, so there will be distinction in reward, when we enter heaven . . . For as Jesus said, "In my Father's house are many dwelling places" (John 14:2, NASB)—and the place He will provide for each of us will be more wonderful than our eyes have ever seen. . . .

But it is more wonderful to think on this: We

will all be there to stand before the great throne—or more likely to kneel in reverent worship—when the Son presents the fruit of His labors to the Father.

For as Paul has told us: "For He must reign until He has put all His enemies under His feet" (1 Corinthians 15:25, NASB). And we will be there in the moment when Death is swallowed up in Life, as Christ presents His Kingdom to the Father.

Then we will stand and begin to serve in our new lives in the Kingdom. Death will be as a nightmare that is past and done. And as we rise to our feet, we who are among the just will already have forgotten how to die.

Irenaeus,
AGAINST THE HERESIES

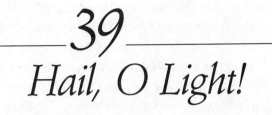

39
Hail, O Light!

The people walking in darkness have seen a great light;
on those living in the land of the shadow of death
a light has dawned.

———

Isaiah 9:2

Jesus said, "I am the light of the world.
Whoever follows me will never walk in darkness,
but will have the light of life."

———

John 8:12

Hail, O Light!

Light from above shone on us while we were prisoners, chained in the dark shadows of Death— Light, purer than the rays of the sun, and sweeter than the fragrant airs that play across the meadows of earth.

You—O Light—are Life everlasting. Everyone who comes out from their darkness to walk in you will share in your life.

Those who are of the night hide from you. The

thought of you makes their soul fear. But night gives way to the Day of your Dawning, Lord. All things, and all men, lie exposed beneath your rising Light.

You, yourself, are the Light of Day, for those of us who are new creatures in you. You are our Sun of justice. You pass over the whole earth, by your Spirit, as you run your course. Your justice visits every one of us, sifting our hearts, exposing our remaining shadows to your Light to free us. For your Father makes His sun to rise upon all alike. And after His light and heat exposes, He comforts us, sending the cooling dew of His Truth. (See Psalm 19.)

For your Father has changed the place of our sun's setting—that is, death—into the place of our new sunrise. Death becomes the dawn of Life! By your death on the cross, O Light, you have snatched men from hell, and have given us a sure place in heaven. . . .

For us who believe, you even transform earth into the bright borderlands of heaven. . . .

Clement of Alexandria,
THE LOGOS, OUR TEACHER

40

He Reigns Forever

[J esus said,] ". . . the sign of the Son of Man will appear in the sky. . . . [The whole earth] will see the Son of Man coming on the clouds of the sky, with power and great glory. And he will send his angels with a loud trumpet call, and they will gather his elect from the four winds, from one end of the heavens to the other. . . . I tell you the truth. . . . Heaven and earth will pass away, but my words will never pass away."

Matthew 24:30–31, 34–35

J esus *will* return from heaven with blazing glory. That is certain.

The prophets proclaim His coming—for when the Son of Man comes, all eyes will see Him in the clouds of heaven, with an army of angels at His command.

It was given to Daniel to look into the future, and he said with astonishment,

"I looked, and there before me was one like a son of man, coming with the clouds of heaven. He approached the Ancient of Days and was led into His presence. He was

given authority, glory and sovereign power; all peoples,
nations and men of every language worshiped him. His
dominion is an everlasting dominion that will not pass
away, and his kingdom is one that will never be destroyed"
(Daniel 7:13–14).

The apostles, and Jesus himself, were careful to
show us how true and certain is the Spirit of
prophecy. They showed us how all the things that
were proclaimed before Christ have been fulfilled.
And so, we must believe that all the prophecies
about things to come will most certainly be fulfilled
as well.

It does not matter whether the world accepts the
word about Christ's second coming. For unbelief
must have its time.

But it will happen one day, when no one
suspects. . . . Suddenly, the whole earth will hear a
mighty shout, and Christ will come down with an
angelic host. Everyone who has ever lived will
come to life again. . . .

Even the prophet Ezekiel saw this long ago. He
was astounded, and cried, "Joint will come together
with joint, and bone with bone, and flesh will grow
again." (See Ezekiel 37.)

Likewise Isaiah peered ahead through time, to
the end of earthly days, and he declared, "Every
knee will bow to the Lord, and every tongue will
confess him!" (See Isaiah 45:23.)

And so I urge you, brothers. Be faithful and
patient every day . . . until the day we long for shall
come. Though our eyes have seen Him not, then we

shall see Him as He is. And though the life we now have from above is but a seed . . . a whispered promise . . . then it shall spring up to eternal life!

For He will gather us to himself—the Lord of Life!—and we will see Him *face to face*.

Even so, Lord Jesus—*come*!

Justin Martyr,
FIRST APOLOGY

DAVID HAZARD developed the REKINDLING THE INNER FIRE devotional series to encouarge others to keep the "heart" of their faith alive and afire with love for God. He also feels a special need to help Christians of today to "meet" men and women of the past whose experience of God belongs to the whole Church, for all the ages.

Hazard is an award-winning writer, the author of books for both adults and children, with international bestsellers among his many titles. He lives in northern Virginia with his wife, MaryLynne, and three children: Aaron, Joel and Sarah Beth.